I0130752

U.K. Chapter of Computer Applications and Quantitative Methods in Archaeology

Proceedings of the Fourth Meeting
Cardiff University, 27 and 28 February 1999

Edited by

Caitlin Buck, Vicky Cummings, Cole Henley, Steve Mills and Steve Trick

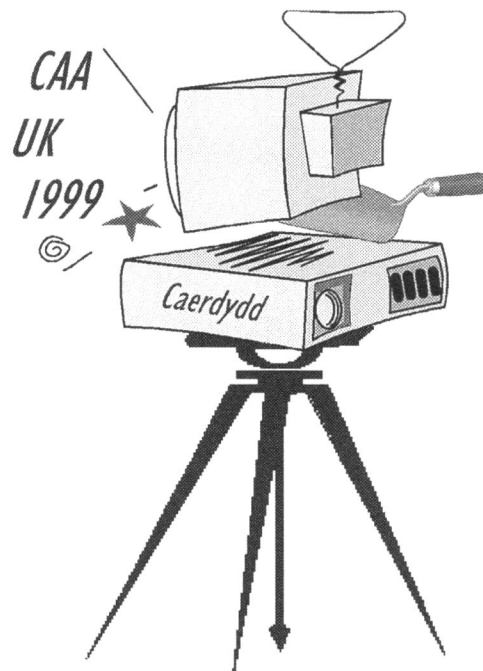

BAR International Series 844
2000

Published in 2019 by
BAR Publishing, Oxford

BAR International Series 844

U.K. Chapter of Computer Applications and Quantitative Methods in Archaeology

© the editors and contributors severally and the publisher 2000

The author's moral rights under the 1988 UK Copyright,
Designs and Patents Act are hereby expressly asserted.

All rights reserved. No part of this work may be copied, reproduced, stored,
sold, distributed, scanned, saved in any form of digital format or transmitted
in any form digitally, without the written permission of the Publisher.

ISBN 9781841710488 paperback
ISBN 9781407351797 e-book
DOI https://doi.org/10.30861/9781841710488

BAR Publishing is the trading name of British Archaeological Reports (Oxford) Ltd.
British Archaeological Reports was first incorporated in 1974 to publish the BAR
Series, International and British. In 1992 Hadrian Books Ltd became part of the BAR
group. This volume was originally published by Archaeopress in conjunction with
British Archaeological Reports (Oxford) Ltd / Hadrian Books Ltd, the Series principal
publisher, in 2000. This present volume is published by BAR Publishing, 2016.

BAR
PUBLISHING

BAR titles are available from:

BAR Publishing
122 Banbury Rd, Oxford, OX2 7BP, UK
EMAIL   info@barpublishing.com
PHONE   +44 (0)1865 310431
FAX   +44 (0)1865 316916
www.barpublishing.com

Contents

Preface

It is with great pleasure that I write the preface to this volume that records contributions made at the fourth meeting of the U.K. Chapter of Computer Applications and Quantitative Methods in Archaeology (CAA) held at Cardiff University on 27 and 28 February 1999. The meeting was notable for the high standard of presentations made and the wide range of subjects covered and I am pleased to say that this is reflected in the papers herein.

The U.K. chapter of CAA was founded in the hope of attracting student delegates and researchers from U.K. field units who find attending international meetings difficult. This hope has been fulfilled and at the 1999 meeting we had a total of almost 100 delegates many of whom were young people attending a CAA meeting for the first time. The 1999 meeting had the added bonus that several of the local student organisers were amongst those attending for the first time. Their enthusiasm and commitment to archaeology is marked and gave rise to many hours of work both before and during the conference to see that things ran smoothly. Without their support the conference would not have been the lively, friendly and successful event it was.

As if this were not enough, the same students readily agreed to help produce a proceedings volume of some of the papers from the meeting. The fact that this collection of papers is before you today is a tribute to their hard work and reliability. Every part of the production of the volume was a true collaboration between the editors whose names appear on the cover. During much of the time that editing was taking place I was in New Zealand on sabbatical and the student editors worked cooperatively and with enormous enthusiasm to see the project through to completion. Electronic communication is a wonderful thing, but people with high spirits and a love of their discipline are more wonderful still!

The editors are greatly indebted to a large number of anonymous referees who read the papers during the editorial process. Each paper was read by at least two members of the research community and, without exception, their comments were apposite, detailed and constructive. I'm sure that all the authors will want to echo my thanks to these individuals.

I really hope that you enjoy reading the papers gathered here and, if you were at the meeting, I trust that it helps invoke happy memories of a weekend spent in Cardiff.

With thanks to all who came to the meeting!

Caitlin Buck
Chair of the Organising Committee
CAA(UK)99

The sigillographic database: an example of easier artefact analysis

Eric Cooper

St. John's College

Oxford, OX1 3JP

United Kingdom

email: eric.cooper@sjc.ox.ac.uk

1 Introduction

In this paper I discuss the potential for adopting electronic database management to aid in sigillographic research, or the study of Byzantine document seals. To those who are well acquainted with computers and their potential applications, much of what I will say in this Introduction may be obvious. But for those not very familiar with computers, a basic awareness of their potential must be formed. During the end of 1997, I created a very modest database while working on an essay. While in discussion with my tutor (Dr. James Howard-Johnston), the topic of electronic databases naturally arose. I say 'naturally', but that is misleading, for I was surprised to hear my tutor comment that no collection of Byzantine document seals had ever been fully catalogued (and made publicly available) in an electronic medium. (I should note that the sigillographic collection of Birmingham University may by now be catalogued on CD-ROM (Dunn pers. comm.). However I know neither if it is publicly available, nor what format it takes.) Only a few months later, a scholar told me that he had always used books for his studies, which had satisfied his needs. The loss of the book would be a shame and degradation to scholarship, and besides it would be too difficult to replace the book with the computer. But, with all due respect, I believe he missed the point. The objective is not to rid ourselves of all books *ad hoc*, but rather to replace them when there is some other tool that is superior. It was these two conversations that inspired the present project.

The following is based on the paper I presented at the CAA (UK) '99 conference at Cardiff. While the general topics herein are the same as those presented at the conference, some of the findings specific to Byzantine studies have been removed for two reasons. First, access to data from 12 unpublished seals (Howard-Johnston pers. comm.) unavailable to me before the conference has subsequently refuted many of my statements and hypotheses. Second, it is envisaged that the primary readership here would not find the material of as much interest as a more extended discussion on the computer-related aspects. It must be stressed from the outset that this paper reports on work in progress. The goal is to highlight a few of the challenges involved in utilising the traditional paper media, for example catalogue books, and some of the advantages of a computer database in the study of Byzantine lead seals. Furthermore, it is hoped that other Byzantinists, in particular, will be stimulated to further exploration of the topic at hand. This paper is based on my current efforts to create a user-friendly database of Byzantine lead seals; limitations have been imposed owing to the early stage of this project, and the fact that I am not a professional computer programmer, but rather am learning as my research proceeds. The following discussion is divided into five basic parts:

1. Introduction and background of Byzantine seals.

2. Traditional research practices and their limitations.

3. Advantages of an electronic database and short case study.

4. Technical issues.

5. Conclusion.

Note that Sections 2, 3 and 4 are addressed primarily to those readers who are not very familiar

1

with computers, and database software in particular. While Section 5 is aimed at those who are knowledgeable about computer databases.

2 Background

Byzantine Studies is still a rather obscure field; unfortunately, the word *Byzantium* itself often draws a blank expression (or one of fear and boredom at any social event) from the general public. The word *Byzantine*, however, is often recognised—invariably from the phrase 'Byzantine bureaucracy' (for more about the bureaucracy, see Oikonomidès 1972). The reason for this may not be obvious *prima facie* since Byzantium is often noted by scholars for its mosaics, churches and distinctive art. It was also the champion of (Greek) Orthodoxy and the shield of Christianity against the Muslim expansion for quite some time (for example see Ramsay 1906; Krautheimer 1965; Kennedy 1979; Haldon and Kennedy 1980; Meyendorff 1983; Geanakoplos 1984; Mango 1986; Laiou and Maguire 1992; Cormack 1998). Be that as it may, the Byzantine administrative apparatus was remarkably sophisticated and effective for its time. The range of court titles and administrative, ecclesiastic, and military offices was always substantial, and it grew as time progressed (compare the lists of precedence in Bury 1911 and Oikonomidès 1972), and the study of Glykatzi-Ahrweiler (1960). Although, or perhaps because, Constantinople was the centre of the Empire, numerous functionaries were in the provinces attending to the needs of the Crown. Furthermore, as Byzantium adapted its organisational structure in response to a changing world (for example the advent of the Arab invasions) military and civil-administrative headquarters increased in number throughout the empire to facilitate more rapid and flexible governmental response to any situation (for example see Whittow 1996, 118–24, 324–5, 344–5). Meanwhile, the Church continued to function and attempted to extend itself beyond the borders of the empire (Shepard 1998, 176–80). Numerous dioceses existed throughout the empire, and monasteries of various sizes and means were scattered from the periphery all the way to the City of Cities, Constantinople (Mango 1994, 105–24; Morris 1985, 185–7).

Effective communication was essential for the coherent direction of all the civil, military and religious offices and sub offices. In Byzantium that effective communication came in the form of writing. We should probably envisage functionaries in the field writing dispatches to superiors; administrative centres sending memoranda internally and externally; military units tracking logistics and transmitting orders; priests and bishops sending communiqués and letters to one another; and a host of others sending information for a variety of reasons. Virtually all of these documents, however, have been lost to us, for they were written on papyrus, parchment, and eventually paper. Though we do not have the documents themselves, we are still able to gain a small glimpse of the information they might have contained.

It is here that the study of Byzantine document seals, i.e. sigillography, offers Byzantinists an important source of information on trade (Antoniadis-Bibicou 1963; Oikonomidès 1986), administration (Antoniadis-Bibicou 1963; Howard-Johnston 1995), prosopography (drawing relationships between various characters in a specific historical context) (Seibt 1976), and so on. (The term *sealing* is here more correct than *seal*. However, I shall follow the popular convention of referring to sealings as seals.) Seals from the medieval world came in various forms, but we are interested here in seals made of lead or gold, the types that are meant when the term *seal* is encountered.

Seals greatly resemble coins (see Figure 1); they have similar shape, size, and sometimes mass. Furthermore, certain decorative elements are common to both. Seals, however, were used as a fastening device, wherein a document was secured by a wire tying the document together in a certain fashion. The seal acted as a clamp holding the two ends of the wire together. This was achieved by taking two flat blanks (the terms tokens or flans may provide a better mental picture) and sandwiching them over the wire's ends. Next, a pliers-like device called a boulloterion was employed (with the help of a striking hammer) to press the two blanks into one whole. A pattern was impressed on both faces of the newly formed seal, much in the way a coin takes a pattern on its faces (see Morrisson 1987, especially p.6f., for picture of a boulloterion).

Seals acted not only as a security device to ensure privacy for the document, but also to verify the document's origin (for uses and types of seals, see Vikan and Nesbitt 1980, especially pp. 5–20). Thus, seals usually contained several important categories of information: the sender's name, office(s) and court title(s); the province, city or territory of the sender; and sometimes other direct information—including dates. All of these

Figure 1: Illustration of a Byzantine Seal (Schlumberger 1883).

data categories hold an obvious significance, and thus have always been included in publications. Seals also contain another group of potentially useful data, which is more indirect in nature. Examples include artistic motifs, iconic representations, monograms, and epigraphic variety. Because some of the more indirect data categories are largely unstudied, one finds that the amount of detailed treatment they receive varies from publication to publication. For example, one now commonly finds listings of all the saints depicted in seal obverses within the respective catalogue. However, one rarely—if ever—finds details tabulated such as the size of the saint depicted or artistic style(s) used. Sigillographic publications will often contain some of this type of information in each individual seal entry, but it is rarely tabulated in convenient charts or indexes.

3 Traditional methods and problems

It is here that we must consider how sigillography has traditionally been conducted. Of course, the ideal would be to have access to all seal archives, but such has never been the case for at least the vast majority of sigillographers. Instead, catalogues, supplements, and journal articles have been published. During the past century, the paper medium has certainly allowed us to conduct research and make advances that we would not have been possible without it, but (as we will see) it is by no means ideal. Paper-based publications require significant physical resources, and are therefore expensive, especially when print runs are short. Thus, more modestly funded institutions have not always been able to acquire all of the sigillographic publications. Moreover, the quality of plates and illustrations is often neglected in order to make the final product more affordable; some catalogues contain no pictures whatsoever (for example Konstantopoulos 1917). Pictures of the seals are often found at the very

end of the catalogue in plates, or sometimes in completely separate volumes (for example Zacos and Veglery 1972). But when the pictures are placed next to their textual entries in the catalogues, it then becomes very difficult to compare them to any other seal not also on that page (for example Nesbitt and Oikonomidès 1996). No single format is ideal. Indexes can only reveal that information which the composer has seen fit to include. Lastly, there is no way in which to correct a mistake once publication has occurred, save by issuing a separate sheet of errata or an update volume (for example seal #161 in Laurent 1962 and seal #659 in Laurent 1932). What is more, there are some physical aspects pertaining to a conventional catalogue that might not be given due consideration until one is actually faced with the situation.

Oddly enough, it seems that one rarely anticipates logistical issues imposed by books. For example, *Byzantine Lead Seals*, Volume I.1 (Zacos and Veglery 1972) is 30 cm tall, 50 cm wide (opened) and 6 cm thick. Now, if one needs to compare the data from several such volumes at once, the amount of space needed just to have all the books open becomes substantial. This may seem trivial at first, but considering that as many as six books might be open in order to study just three seals, keeping track of where each specific seal is, what it looks like compared to the others, and so on, becomes tiresome. Moreover, comparing fine details about seals depicted in low-resolution images—or even hand-drawn—in several books can be very difficult, especially when the alternative could be to have the pictures laid out next to each other at very high resolution and at any zoom-factor desired. Also, seal catalogues are often confined to libraries; if one needs catalogues located in more than one library, research can become difficult and time consuming. There is the additional point that travelling with a library of sigillographic catalogues is almost always impracticable; one cannot conduct research while away from a fully furnished

3

library, nor even consult a reference while one is in the field. At a guess, there are some 70,000 to 100,000 seals known through publication. Thus, one can imagine the extensive library needed to study the subject (for example the bibliography in Nesbitt and Oikonomidès 1996).

4 Electronic Databases

While the majority of those who attended the CAA (UK) '99 conference may not need to be persuaded about the advantages of electronic databases for the analysis of artefacts such as Byzantine lead seals, very little nevertheless has been done by Byzantinists themselves in this regard. As far as I am aware, the earliest electronic database, and the only one other than my own (and possibly Birmingham, see above), was created in early 1980 (for details about this early database, see Lounghis 1990). An electronic sigillographic database at that time was certainly at the cutting edge of implementing technology for Byzantine studies. However, little appears to have been done since then, and no further versions or upgrades seem to have been undertaken. The lack of interest may be due to the nature of the interface. That is, interaction with the database was done solely through the use of numeric codes. One could not query by entering a string search (for example 'Cappadocia'), but only via a numeric key. Every office, province, name, and so on had a specific numeric representation. As I understand it, the results of queries are also returned numerically, i.e. without words. Thus, one must interact with the database completely via a non-intuitive code that requires a chart for decryption.

This observation is not a criticism of those who created the database, but merely recognition of the technological limitations of the time. Furthermore, the fact that the earlier database could only store alphanumeric data made it inferior to paper media in many regards. Not only are books more intuitive to use than a program operated by complex codes, but books can hold illustrations and special fonts that could not be included in the earlier database.

The last few years, however, have seen one of the most significant advances in database design: that user interfaces are (or should be) much more logical and friendly to the user. With the proliferation of graphical interfaces, one may now create and use a database with sensible text and icon interaction. Furthermore, objects such as pictures, sound, and video can now all be incorporated in a single database. The advances in database theory and design have also increased the power of the computer database: a relational database allows for extremely complex data associations and management, and is far more versatile than the more primitive flat-file database. In the most basic terms, a relational database holds data pertaining to one item in separate tables, thus providing great flexibility in what data one may compare, whereas a flat-file database must contain all data about an item in one table. A spreadsheet may be considered a flat-file database for convenience (see below for more precise definition). The cost of the equipment needed to utilise a computerised database is now at the level where Western families of modest means can afford an adequate system. Thus, modern technology offers us a superior alternative to the paper medium.

My own project is still in its earliest stages, but has already shown great potential. The hardware platform is a laptop computer with an Intel Pentium II 266MHz processor and 4 GB hard disk; images were acquired through various low-end scanners. The database is stored in Microsoft's Access 97 (see Table 1 for the URL). As a result, creation of the entire database did not, require substantial resources, and even fewer resources are needed by those who simply wish to make use of it. At present, some 500 lead seals have been entered into the database, of which just 22 have associated images that are not protected by copyright. The entire database footprint is under 1.5 MB, but will certainly increase with each additional entry and the inclusion of a specialised editorial font currently under construction.

Logistics aside, certain aspects about the database need to be mentioned. Some basic computer literacy is required: all computer novices who tried my database were unable to operate it effectively. It is my plan, however, that few people will encounter any significant difficulty once I implement an improved interface and include a help utility. In the meantime, for the purposes of my own research, the flexibility of the computer database has already proven far superior, and preferable, to the book. For example, there are numerous seals that have been published whose original proposed dates now need revision. Obviously, in book format one would need to publish a supplemental catalogue with all the revisions. The reader then needs to remember to consult that tome in addition to the earlier publication(s). In fact, it is more likely that several different publications would result, at least one for each collection. With the elec-

Software	URL	Accessed
Access	http://www.microsoft.com/	1/3/00
SQL Server	http://www.microsoft.com/	1/3/00
ORACLE	http://www.oracle.com/	1/3/00
Paradox	http://www.corel.com/	1/3/00
Alpha Five	http://alphasoftware.com/	1/3/00
R:BASE	http://microrim.com/	1/3/00
Visual FoxPro	http://www.microsoft.com/	1/3/00
dBASE	http://www.dbase2000.com/	1/3/00
Visual Basic	http://www.microsoft.com/	1/3/00

Table 1: URLs of software cited in the text.

tronic database, however, it is a simple matter of replacing all the pertinent data and including notes about each change in the respective seal's memo field.

What happens when an author discovers the need to include a data category *after the publication has been made*? A similar situation arose when Nicolas Oikonomidès examined lead seal blanks and thought of a new category relevant to all sigillographic publications (Oikonomidès 1987). In the paper world a modified reprint or a special supplement will have to be created. The first option may be too costly for all parties concerned; the second option may prove too awkward to use efficiently. But in a computer database, new fields can be added and updates performed relatively easily. Over time, it became apparent that two fields not originally in my database were needed. The first was a yes/no field detailing whether a seal had been overstruck; the second field recorded any misspellings found in the original inscription. Minimal time was needed to restructure the database and re-integrate all of the data. Thus, the database can be expanded, updated or otherwise changed and still remain a coherent entity.

The flexibility and efficiency of the electronic database combined with extraordinary speed saved me significant amounts of time. As an experiment, I kept track of the time it took me to conduct research and to produce charts for all of the Byzantine lead seals pertaining to a region in present-day Turkey called Cappadocia. The total number of seals found in publications was 51; information for 12 other unpublished seals was also included (mentioned above).

When using paper records, the time spent collating and charting various information about the distribution of seals per century, different titles and ranks, number and breakdown of iconic obverses, types and distributions of seals in each collection, and a comparison with the finds from another Byzantine province (the Anatolikon) was five hours. The time mentioned here only covers the that taken to sort through all my notes and create rough charts.

Once the electronic database was created, I used the software tools to undertake the same task. I was able to tabulate the different first and last names with their distribution over time and the geographical breakdown in both find provenance and place of issue whenever possible. The total time taken was under half an hour, including the creation of separate charts for each query. I then colour printed all of the charts and a catalogue-style report for someone else to peruse, in an additional 15 minutes (see Figure 2, for example).

I should point out here that printing up a paper report does not invalidate my arguments for a computerised database. Rather, I was able to produce a completely customised report with high-resolution colour illustrations at a fraction of the cost of a standard publication for a person who did not have a computer. At any time, changes can be made and a new, updated report printed in moments. Moreover, the paper copy was not a replacement of the entire database, but a 'snapshot' of the results of a query. Such 'snapshots' cannot readily be created from traditional paper publications on demand.

5 Technical Issues

Now, constructing a sigillographic database that will meet the needs of scholars requires much forethought and planning. First, let us consider why Access 97 (hereafter called simply Access) was used (please see Table 1 for the associated URL of this database, and of all other software mentioned in this section). Perhaps the most significant factor at the moment involves how the

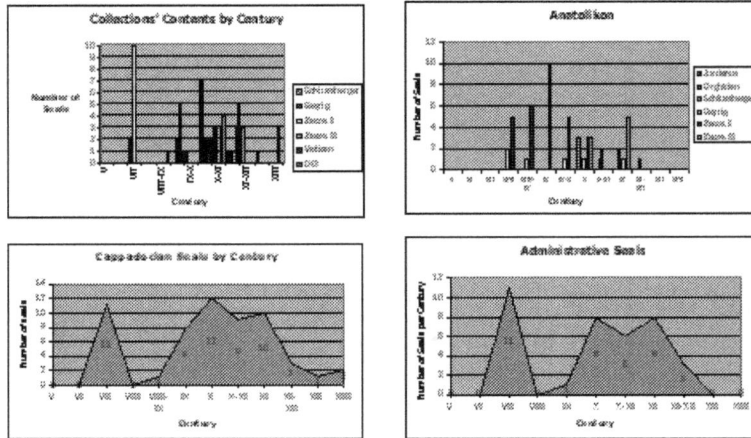

Figure 2: Basic charts of (clockwise) Collections, the Anatolikon, Cappadocia, and Administrative distributions.

database and data are to be disseminated. Because there are numerous collections of Byzantine seals, it will be difficult—if not impossible—to create a single, unified database: issues of licensing, remuneration, acknowledgement and even ownership may all arise. The issue of copyright is especially problematic, for it is not yet clear in international law who holds the copyright of an image displayed on the World-Wide-Web—he who possesses the physical item, or he who displays the image on the Internet (Nesbitt 1997). Thus, it seems more likely that individual collections would publish their sigillographic holdings on CD-ROM or DVD, say, rather than allow them to be displayed on the Internet by a centralised server (at least until such legal problems have been resolved).

There are obvious reasons why one would desire the database to be Web-accessible, and thus Web-accessibility should ultimately be a goal. The back-end Relational Database Management System (RDBMS) could thus be something along the lines of Microsoft SQL Server or an ORACLE system, benefiting from a powerful, fully dedicated server. Platform independence would therefore be achieved, and users of various operating systems such as Apple, Windows, Linux, Unix, and BeOs would not require separate software applications. Plus, only a very modest, net-enabled platform would be required for the end-user, as the backend platform would do the real work. It becomes more exciting when one considers that soon palmtops and other very small devices may be able to interface with such a system—fieldwork would be greatly advantaged. A distributed database, i.e. data tables located on multiple servers, might be realised sooner, be-

cause individual collections would still maintain control over their respective holdings. But even that will still be a long time in coming. It is beyond our scope here to delve more into the issues of who might administer the database, edit the seals, and so on.

As already stated, sigillographic databases for individual platforms/users may be more readily realisable. I envisage separate collections publishing sigillographic databases on CD-ROM or DVD that all conform to a yet-to-be-determined standard, both in terms of format/metadata (see Figure 3) and relational database management system (RDBMS); they would in essence plug in seamlessly with whatever other sigillographic databases are already present on the machine. It was with the considerations just mentioned and for the reasons following that I chose to use Access, which would be my recommendation for which RDBMS to use at the moment. First, Access has the only 'complete' database file structure, (i.e. a complete database including forms, queries, reports, and so on) which can be stored in a single .mdb file (Jennings 1997, 115). Therefore, sigillographic database(s) can be created that do not require other applications to manipulate and view the data; the application will be completely self-contained. Second, the variable-length record structure of data rows in Access is more efficient than fixed-length record structure such as is found in xBase; therefore Access can often create smaller files. The way in which Access stores data, i.e. uses headers and pointers in 2-KB pages, means that it is much faster than the INSERT method of xBase or Paradox (Jennings 1997, 812). The versatility in importing/exporting file types is also greater

6

than several other database applications of similar size/scope, for example Alpha Five 3 Professional Edition and R:BASE 6.1 for Windows (Gleidman 1998). This versatility is crucial, primarily because tables formed in Access can be ported easily to any server-based SQL RDBMS, as long as there is an Open Database Connectivity (ODBC) Application Programming Interface (API) driver available; most major client/server DBMSs provide ODBC drivers (Jennings 1997, 904–905). Access can, of course, also be used to import/export various other database file types such as Paradox, FoxPro, and dBASE. Thus, Access seems to be a good choice for commencing a sigillographic database. It can be used to create complete object-enabled database applications in relatively small footprints that serve both as backend and frontend and, when desirable or appropriate, it can be converted easily to a more robust server/client SQL RDBMS.

On the ANSI/SPARC (American National Standards Institute/Standards Planning and Requirements Committee) conceptual level, two main, interrelated points must be noted. First, data independence, defined by Date (Date 1990, 18) as 'the immunity of applications to change in storage structure and access technique', must be sought as far as possible. This can be achieved partly by storing only data entities in a file. That is, the file should contain only stored table occurrences and not other objects such as queries, forms, reports, or program modules; the other objects can be stored together in a separate file (Jennings 1997, 779). Thus, compatibility among different versions of Access is enhanced, and conversion to most other database systems is (theoretically) very straightforward. Second, the data must be normalised—to at least the First Normal Form (1NF), but preferably as high as the Fifth Normal Form (5NF). 1NF may be defined as the condition that all underlying named sets of scalar values of a relation contain only atomic values (Date 1990, 251, 533). It is easier, however, to think of 1NF as requiring tables that have only rows and columns (or records and fields), and data cells cannot contain more than one value (Jennings 1997, 789). The database must achieve at least 1NF in order to be a relational database (Date 1990, 559) as well as have data independence. For purposes of efficiency, 3NF—all non-key columns of a table depend on the table's primary key (Jennings 1997, 791)—is the desired minimum. Whether or not the database should surpass 3NF will depend on the content of the final, agreed set of fields (see Date 1990, 559–60).

The last issue I would like to mention is that

of image storage. Obviously, pictures of the seals are images, but the inscriptions in Byzantine Greek and the very specialised editorial font will need to be too, because neither script is supported in ASCII or Unicode. What storage format should be used? At first thought, one might favour the use of an object-oriented file format such as Encapsulated PostScript. Resizing object-oriented graphics does not distort them or make them fuzzy; however they lack a universally editable file format (Blatner *et al.* 1998, 46–7). Instead, we need to use bitmap file formats, of which three appear most suitable for our purposes: TIFF, PNG (Portable Network Graphic, pronounced 'ping'), and FlashPix. TIFF (Tagged Image File Format) is still considered by Blatner *et al.* (1998, 59) 'the best way to store single-resolution, device-targeted . . . lossless color bitmaps' because of the comprehensive features it provides.

Of all industry standard bitmap formats, TIFF is the most widely used: almost every program that works with bitmaps can handle TIFF images (Blatner *et al.* 1998, 49). In fact, there is only one drawback with TIFF, to wit it does not display in a Web browser (Blatner *et al.* 1998, 50). PNG, however, does display in a browser and offers numerous features including lossless compression but not CMYK (Cyan Magenta Yellow blacK) colour model support, which may be an issue when colour printing is desired; as time progresses, it is probable that the majority of Web browsers will support this format (Blatner *et al.* 1998, 55–56). PNG is also the native graphic format for Access 97—actually all Microsoft Office 97 applications (Jennings 1997, 686). FlashPix is still too new for us to determine whether or not it will catch on or become 'vapour ware', but the fact that nearly every company that develops imaging software has stated it will support the format suggests it will succeed (Blatner *et al.* 1998, 56–9). One notable advantage of FlashPix format is that the files are stored in such a fashion (multiple sample blocks) that low-end systems can display and manipulate the images easily. The downside, however, is that lossless compression is not yet available—though a compression format similar to LZW may be added soon (Blatner *et al.* 1998, 57–60). So, which one to choose? I would suggest at least two of the formats, TIFF and PNG. Since the fate of FlashPix is still so uncertain, it seems premature to rely on this format, especially since it lacks compression. However, if we link the images to the database rather than embed them, then one can choose to install only the TIFF format of each image,

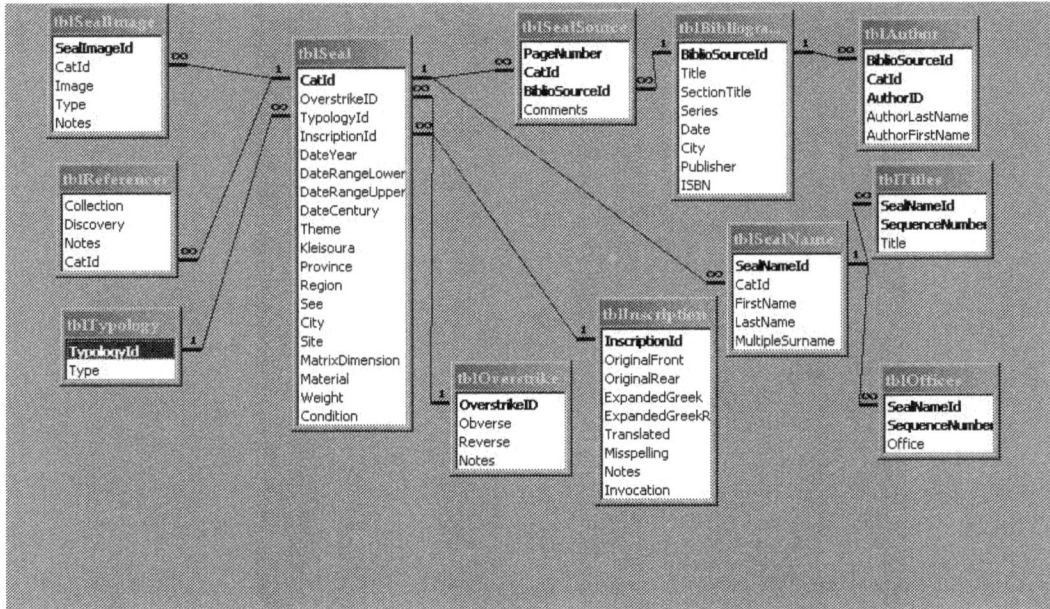

Figure 3: Relations, tables, and fields.

PNG format, or both. The use of absolute paths instead of relative paths by Access can be circumvented by the use of Microsoft Visual Basic code, allowing flexibility in where and how the images are stored (Bell pers. comm.). Thus, maximum versatility is ensured—one can print any image in the database using any current colour printer, and also display images on the Web (if and when appropriate).

6 Conclusion

In brief, I hope this cursory discussion has illustrated some of the potential of a sigillographic database. The superior flexibility, adaptability, and efficiency of the electronic database compared to the more traditional methods employed in sigillography have now been demonstrated. Of course, the current project is certainly not the end, but rather the very beginning; I make no pretence that my meagre database is in any way complete. Certainly, the questions and issues raised here are only the tip of the iceberg: sigillographers need to come together and discuss what the database should be able to do—and hence what fields should ultimately be included. This in turn will determine how the data are to be structured. Dissemination of the material needs also to be addressed, for example Web-based or CD-ROM. Once these issues are resolved, we will then be able to move on to topics not covered here at all, such as maintenance and updating.

Needless to say, there is so much more to do. Hopefully, discussion will now turn from whether an electronic sigillographic database has anything to offer and is practicable, to how can we can best devise one, what conventions should be employed, and so on. We need to recognise the advantages posed by using computerised systems and explore how we may capitalise upon them. The transition will require effort and time, but the returns will greatly aid the advancement of the field.

References

[1] Antoniadis-Bibicou, H. 1963. *Recherches sur les Douanes a Byzance.* Paris, Librairie Armand Colin.

[2] Blatner, D., Fleishman, G. and Roth, S. 1998. *Real World Scanning and Halftones: the definitive guide to scanning and halftones from the desktop.* Berkeley, Peachpit Press.

[3] Bury, J. B. 1911. *The Imperial Administrative System in the Ninth Century.* New York, B. Franklin.

[4] Cormack, R. 1998. Away from the centre: 'provincial' art in the Ninth century. In L. Brubaker, (ed.), *Byzantium in the Ninth Century: Dead or Alive?*, pp. 151–66. Aldershot, Variorum.

[5] Date, C. J. 1990. *An Introduction to Database Systems.* Reading, MA, Addison-Wesley.

[6] Geanakoplos, D. J. 1984. *Byzantium: church, society, and civilization seen through contemporary eyes.* Chicago, University of Chicago Press.

[7] Gleidman, J. 1998. Powerhouse Databases. *Computer Shopper Magazine.* (http://www.zdnet.com/products/stories/reviews/0,4161,288515,00.html, Accessed 17/1/00).

[8] Glykatzi-Ahrweiler, H. 1960. Recerces sur l'administration de l'empire Byzantin aux. IXè–XIè siècles. *BCH*, 84:1–109.

[9] Haldon, J. and Kennedy, H. 1980. The Arab-Byzantine Frontier in the Eighth and Ninth Centuries: Military Organisation and Society in the Borderlands. *ZRVI*, 19:79–116.

[10] Howard-Johnston, J. D. 1995. Crown Lands and the Defence of Imperial Authority in the Tenth and Eleventh Centuries. *Byzantinische Forschungen*, 21:75–100.

[11] Jennings, R. 1997. *Special Edition Using Access 97, Second Edition.* Indianapolis, IN: QUE Corporation.

[12] Kennedy, H. 1979. Arab Settlement on the Byzantine Frontier in the Eighth and Ninth Centuries. *Yayla*, 2:22–24.

[13] Konstantopoulos, K. M. 1917. *Βυζαντιακα Μολυβδοβουλλα του εν Αθηναιε Εθνικου Νομισματικου Μουσειου.* Athens, Athens Numismatic Museum. Reprinted from Journal international d'archéologie numismatique 5(1910)–10(1917).

[14] Krautheimer, R. 1965. *Early Christian and Byzantine Architecture.* Harmondsworth, Penguin Books.

[15] Laiou, A. E. and Maguire, H., (eds.) 1992. *Byzantium, A World Civilization.* Washington D.C., Dumbarton Oaks.

[16] Laurent, V. 1932. Les bulles métriques dans la sigillographie Byzantine. *Hellenika.* 4(1931)–8(1938).

[17] Laurent, V. 1962. *Les Sceaux Byzantins du Mèdailler Vatican.* Vatican, Biblioteca Apostolica Vaticana.

[18] Lounghis, T. C. 1990. Researching Seals in a Byzantine Chronography Data Base System. In N. Oikonomidès, (ed.), *Studies in Byzantine Sigillography*, pp. 7–15. Washington D.C., Dumbarton Oaks.

[19] Mango, C. 1986. *Byzantine Architecture.* London, Faber and Faber.

[20] Mango, C. 1994. *Byzantium. The Empire of the New Rome.* London, Phœnix.

[21] Meyendorff, J. 1983. *Byzantine Theology. Historical Trends and Doctrinal Themes.* New York, Fordham University Press.

[22] Morris, R. 1985. Monasteries and Their Patrons in the Tenth and Eleventh Centuries. *Byzantinische Forschungen*, 10:185–232.

[23] Morrisson, C. 1987. Numismatique et Sigillographie: parentes et methode. In N. Oikonomidès, (ed.), *Studies in Byzantine Sigillography*, pp. 1–25. Washington, D.C., Dumbarton Oaks.

[24] Nesbitt, J. 1975. The Office of the Oikistikos: Five Seals in the Dumbarton Oaks Collection. *Dumbarton Oaks Papers*, 29:341–5.

[25] Nesbitt, J. 1977. Double Names on Early Byzantine Lead Seals. *Dumbarton Oaks Papers*, 31:111–123.

[26] Nesbitt, J. 1997. Oxford Colloquium on Byzantine Sigillography and Prosopography. 14 November 1997.

[27] Nesbitt, J. and Oikonomidès, N. 1996. *Catalogue of Byzantine Seals at Dumbarton Oaks and in the Fogg Museum of Art.* Washington, D.C., Dumbarton Oaks.

[28] Oikonomidès, N. 1972. *Les listes de préséance Byzantines des IXe et Xe Siècles: introduction, texte, traduction, commentaire.* Paris, Éditions du Centre national de la Recherche scientifique.

[29] Oikonomidès, N. 1986. Silk Trade and Production in Byzantium from the Sixth to the Ninth Century: the Seals of Kommerkiarioi. *Dumbarton Oaks Papers*, 40:33–50.

[30] Oikonomidès, N. 1987. The Lead Blanks used for Byzantine Seals. In N. Oikonomidès, (ed.), *Studies in Byzantine Sigillography*, pp. 97–104. Washington, D.C., Dumbarton Oaks.

[31] Ramsay, W. M. 1906. The War of Moslem and Christian for the Possession of Asia Minor. In W. M. Ramsay, (ed.), *Studies in the History and Art of the Eastern Roman Provinces*, pp. 281–301. Aberdeen, Aberdeen University Press.

[32] Schlumberger, G. 1883. Sceaux Byzantins. *Revue Archeologique*. Plate X, seal 2.

[33] Seibt, W. 1976. *Die Skleroi: Eine prosopographisch-sigillographische Studie.* Vienna, Verl. d. Österr. Akad. d. Wiss.

[34] Shepard, J. 1998. Byzantine relations with the outside world in the Ninth Century: an introduction. In L. Brubaker, (ed.), *Byzantium in the Ninth Century: Dead or Alive?*, pp. 167–80. Aldershot, Ashgate Publishing Limited.

[35] Vikan, G. and Nesbitt, J. 1980. *Security in Byzantium: Locking, Sealing, and Weighing.* Washington, D.C., Dumbarton Oaks.

[36] Whittow, M. 1996. *The Making of Orthodox Byzantium, 600–1025.* London, Macmillan Press.

[37] Zacos, G. and Veglery, A. 1972. Byzantine Lead Seals. Basel.

Landscapes in motion: interactive computer imagery and the Neolithic landscapes of the Outer Hebrides

Vicky Cummings

School of History and Archaeology
Cardiff University, PO Box 909
Cardiff CF1 3XU, United Kingdom
email: CummingsVM@Cardiff.ac.uk

1 Introduction

In recent years, the role of landscape has come to the forefront of archaeological debate (for example Bender 1993b; Tilley 1994; Nash 1997). It is increasingly widely accepted that the landscape was fundamental to the experiences of the peoples of Neolithic Europe, particularly in relation to the setting of monuments. In this paper I will present initial results arising from fieldwork relating to the Neolithic landscapes of the Outer Hebrides. In doing so, I will consider a selection of techniques that may assist in the analysis and presentation of visual aspects of archaeological landscapes.

It is my opinion

- that there are instances in which digital images are a more effective medium for conveying impressions of place than traditional printed publications, and

- that individual readers of archaeological reports stand to gain greatly from access to digital images, since they can (with appropriate software) 'move' within the image and interpret the evidence for themselves.

As such, this preliminary paper is constrained by presentation via the printed page. A more comprehensive work is in preparation (Cummings 2000) that will, via the use of Apple QTVR (QuickTime Virtual Reality, see Table 1 for the URL) and the World-Wide-Web (WWW), allow readers to observe and manipulate digital images directly. In this paper, I focus on my recent field and laboratory work undertaken to produce such images. I outline the strengths and weaknesses of a selection of approaches and hope to encourage others to consider using digital imagery in landscape studies. I explain how virtual reality images can be created successfully with minimal equipment and at small financial cost.

2 Theoretical approaches to landscape

The importance of experiencing the landscape is being increasingly acknowledged in both prehistoric and historic contexts. It is not my intention to define the term landscape since this matter has been fully discussed elsewhere (Bender 1993b; Tilley 1994). Although archaeologists have talked about the landscape for many years, however, it is only recently that they have begun to look intensively at its role in the context of individual sites (Bender 1992; Bradley 1998a; Kirk 1997; Richards 1996).

2.1 The holistic landscape

One criticism levelled at the concept of landscape is that it seeks to totalise and homogenise human experience (Johnson 1998). Central to this is the possibility that archaeologists may be disregarding their own historically situated and subjective experiences of the landscape in an attempt to present an objective reality. At the same time, it is clear that archaeologists are subject to the same kinds of influences as individuals in the past. Like people throughout time, we are unable to stand back and objectify the landscapes we study or engage with. Landscape is a highly personal experience which is dependent on the specific time and place of encounter, in addition to our own world views and life histories. We also have agendas that will directly affect the way in which we understand and experience archae-

Software/Web resource	URL	Accessed
Apple QTVR	http://quicktime.apple.com	15/02/00
Bodmin Moor Project	http://www.ucl.ac.uk/leskernick/home.htm	15/02/00
SpinPanorama	http://www.pictureworks.com	15/02/00
Paintshop Pro	http://www.jasc.com	15/02/00

Table 1: URLs of software/web resources cited in the text.

ological landscapes (Bender 1998; Darvill 1997). Thus, landscape is inevitably a highly subjective construct, and as such is continually open to a multiplicity of experience and meaning. Manipulation of images using computer software offers us a unique way of expressing this multiplicity of experience, by providing a context for publishing multiple accounts of landscape and enough visual data to allow the reader to interpret the evidence. This will be examined in more detail below.

2.2 The distant landscape

The recognition that all landscapes are experienced subjectively does not evade the implicit object/subject dichotomy also inherent in a postmodern view of the world. The term landscape was first used in the sixteenth century to describe a form of painting, along with a way of altering the earth (landscaping), and consequently implies a fixed relationship between object and subject. This means that the object, in this case the landscape, has been marginalised and distanced in our interpretations (Karlsson 1997). This makes it appear that objects only have meaning when *we* assign them meaning. Thus, landscapes are essentially blank and meaningless *spaces* unless we turn them into named and inhabited *places*. This dichotomy is difficult to deconstruct, although recent attempts have been provided by Thomas (1996) and Karlsson (1997) who utilise the Heideggerian concepts of dwelling and being-in-the-world (Dasein) to nullify the object/subject dualism. Computing can offer little additional assistance to this problem, but this does have interesting implications for the creation and use of hyperspaces and hyperplaces in the landscape of the Internet (Curry 1998).

2.3 The visual landscape

A further drawback with landscape studies is that they privilege vision. The dominance of the visual in the western world also stems back to the sixteenth century and the growth of empiricism, where vision was considered the most

reliable form of representation (Duncan 1993). Since then, vision has become increasingly important in the way we understand our world. Western culture is dominated by the visual and prescribes the way in which we use our eyes and interpret our visual experiences. Landscape studies have been particularly affected by the dominance of vision. Since the term 'landscape' was created to describe a type of painting, it automatically referred to something visual. Initially, landscape studies were primarily carried out by geographers who used maps and other pictorial forms to *represent* the landscape. Since then, we have found other ways to represent the landscape such as aerial photographs and plans, and with the growth of computing in archaeology, multimedia such as GIS and virtual reality. These visual forms let us view the landscape from a viewpoint that is impossible to obtain in reality (see Figures 1 and 2). Haraway (1991) calls this the God-trick: seeing everything from nowhere.

In addition, it has been suggested that we look at the world through a western, male gaze (Thomas 1993; Bender 1993a). This is a fundamental problem within archaeology and the social sciences as a whole, and is difficult to resolve as there is no such thing as passive vision. However, I hope that this paper will begin to address this problem by proposing some alternative forms of visual communication. We must also remember that our encounters with the landscape are not simply visual, but can also be experienced through smell, sound, taste and touch (Rodaway 1994; Tilley 1999). Unfortunately, this is beyond the scope of this paper, although this issue is raised elsewhere (Mills this volume).

2.4 Temporality and the landscape

Another essential element in understanding the concept of landscape is the realisation that it is temporal in nature. To understand and engage with the world requires a sense of time. Places within the landscape are created, named and used through time, and landscapes achieve their identity over time (Chapman 1997). Move-

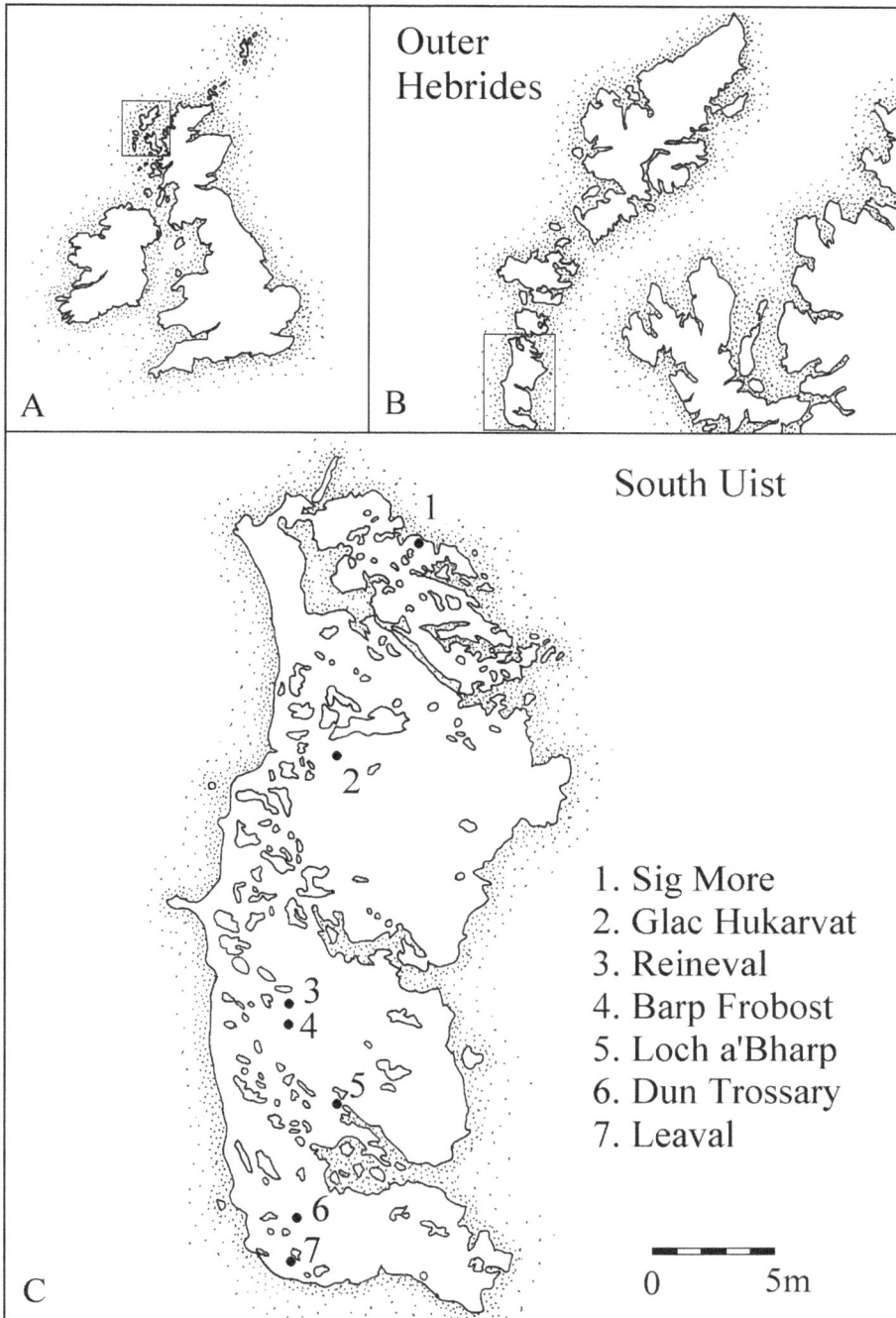

Figure 1: Location map of South Uist.

1. Sig More
2. Glac Hukarvat
3. Reineval
4. Barp Frobost
5. Loch a'Bharp
6. Dun Trossary
7. Leaval

Outer Hebrides

South Uist

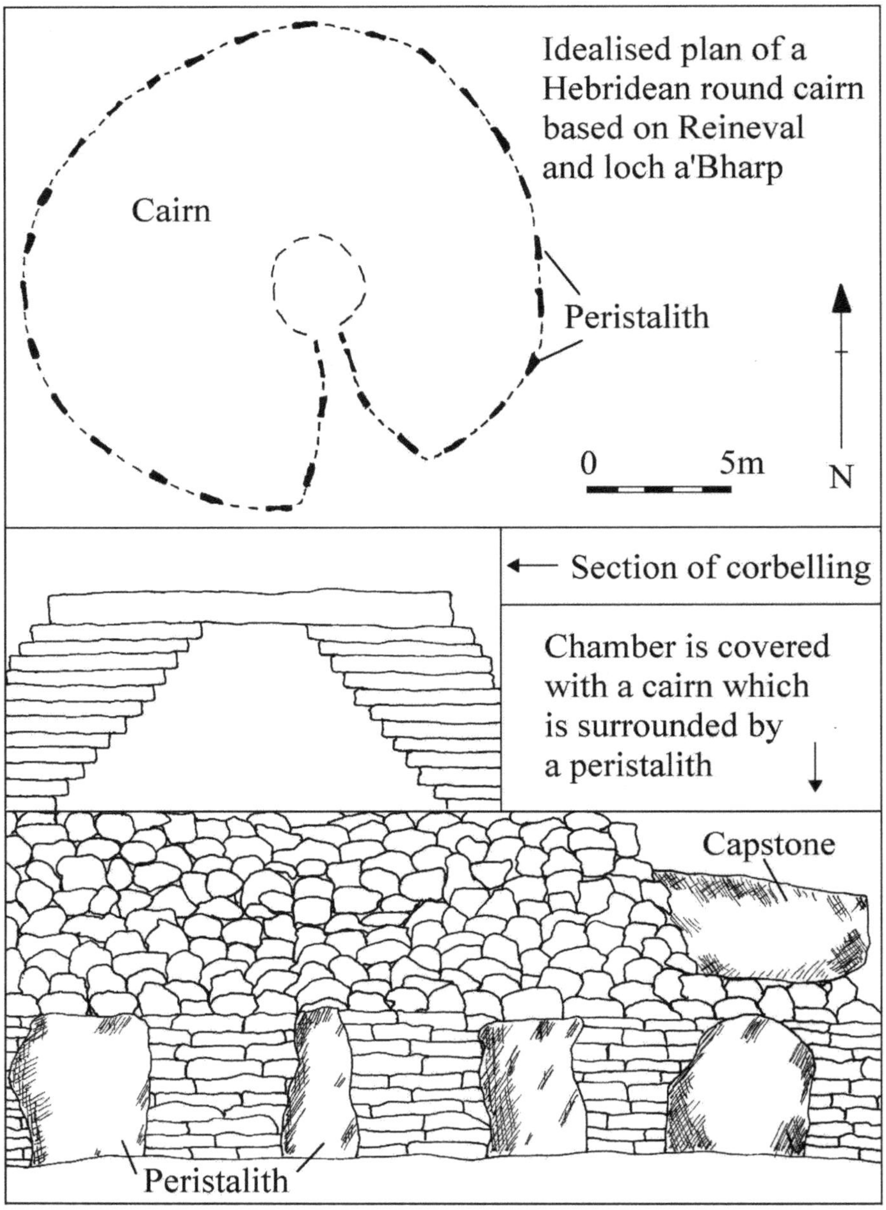
Idealised plan of a
Hebridean round cairn
based on Reineval
and loch a'Bharp
Cairn
Peristalith
0
5m
N
Section of corbelling
Chamber is covered
with a cairn which
is surrounded by
a peristalith
Capstone
Peristalith

Figure 2: An idealised Hebridean round cairn.

ment through the world is movement through both space *and* time (Ingold 1993). This means that landscapes are also never static, but changing from moment to moment. This can be seen at a number of different temporal scales. At one level, the landscape changes over decades, centuries, or millennia. At another it changes dramatically in response to the changing seasons. It can also be transformed daily, or even from minute to minute. Its appearance will depend upon both the weather, and the time of day. Clearly then, time-depth is a fundamental contributor to the experience of landscape. A lack of temporal awareness is one of the key criticisms levelled at techniques such as GIS (Gillings and Goodrick 1996). The methods I will present below also suffer from this drawback, but I hope that in the near future these limitations will be overcome. I will propose ways in which this may be achieved.

2.5 Representing the landscape: previous approaches

Most accounts of landscape use traditional academic writing in their discussion. This is typically in the passive voice and it is the form of writing that we are most familiar with. Almost all discussions on landscape also include some form of artwork, usually black and white photographs along with plans and maps: this is the traditional way in which we add authority to our texts. A classic example is *A phenomenology of landscape* by Christopher Tilley (1994). In chapter five, Tilley describes a walk along the Dorset cursus which is presented alongside a series of photographs taken *en route*. Although this represents a timely and useful contribution to work on landscape, the presentation of these concepts in the format of a printed book fails to adequately convey either a sense of place, or Tilley's own experience of his journey through the landscape. The rectangular, monochrome, photographs provide the reader with a rather abstracted perspective and although we possess a sense of anticipation regarding the subject matter, the combination of visuals and text leaves us with a feeling that Tilley's experience has simply not been communicated adequately. The reader simply fails to gain a sense of the landscape: this is a problem faced by most landscape archaeologists. How do we give the reader a 'feel' for the landscapes in question?

I hope to have shown in this first section that understanding and representing the landscape is problematic for a number of reasons. I have em-

phasised a few of these problems and how they directly affect interpretations of landscape. Many other issues remain to be addressed. However, it is possible to say that landscapes are lived-in, multisensory, embodied and engendered. Landscapes are fluid, temporally situated and open to a multiplicity of experience and meaning. With this in mind, I hope to illustrate how the manipulation of images using computer software may offer effective ways around some of these problems.

3 Representing the landscapes of South Uist

In 1998, a survey of the Neolithic chambered cairns on the isle of South Uist in the Outer Hebrides (Figure 1) was undertaken (Cummings *et al.* forthcoming). The aim was to update Henshall's inventory (Henshall 1972) and to analyse and interpret the landscape settings of these sites. There are six classic Hebridean chambered round cairns known on South Uist (Figure 2), and a single long cairn. They are consistent with other Neolithic cairns in the Western Isles (Armit 1996). Analysis revealed a number of similar themes in the location of the cairns within the landscape. Sites were often built to obscure the view of the flat coastal plain and the coastline to the west, while views of nearby lochs were emphasised. Views of distant mountains to the east were emphasised while views to the west were restricted. In addition, movement around the outside of these cairns was found to dramatically open up or shut down a variety of wide-ranging views, as these monumental sites themselves obscure large portions of the horizon.

When writing up the findings of this fieldwork, the difficulties of conveying an impression of the landscape soon became apparent. Traditional methods of commentary (discussion in the passive voice with black and white photographs, plans and maps) were simply unable to capture the sense of an active and experienced landscape. The three fieldworkers had all observed and interpreted the landscape differently, and this multiplicity of experience was lost in the translation to the printed page. In addition, it seemed likely that people who read the article would want to interpret the evidence for themselves, perhaps in a variety of different ways or to fit into their own research. Consequently, we experimented with creating a more accessible interface between our encounters with the South Uist landscape, and the reader who is less familiar with these places.

Firstly, we were aware that photographs, especially in black and white, are insufficient to reveal the whole landscape setting of a site. Each image represents only a fragment of the whole view. With this is mind, a series of 360 degree line drawings were produced for each site (Figure 3). Previously, this method seems to have been primarily utilised to illustrate views of the landscape in guidebooks, perhaps most famously by Alfred Wainwright in his Pictorial Guides to the English Lake District (Wainwright 1960). Their application in archaeology however, has remained limited, despite there being several advantages with this approach.

1. It allows the reader to gain an impression of the complete landscape setting. In the case of Reineval (Figure 3), the reader can see for themselves which mountains are visible from the site, and also how the façade blocks out the view towards the flat coastal plain and the sea. The reader can also look around the image in their own time, reintroducing an element of spontaneity which is often lost when an image is presented as a framed snapshot.

2. This type of illustration can be easily reproduced in printed form.

3. A number of panoramas can be depicted on a page, allowing landscape settings for groups of sites to be compared. This allows rapid identification of broad themes or similarities in the views.

There are also disadvantages. These viewstrips do not give any real sense of the landscape in terms of scale, distance or temporality. It is difficult to grasp perspective, the view is static, and the reader has to rely upon the decisions of the illustrator as to what the image depicts and what has been omitted. Overall, it remains hard to conceptualise the landscape from this type of image. It is ultimately another visual form which, like maps, can never be seen in reality.

3.1 Landscape and the World-Wide-Web

In order to overcome some of these difficulties, I began to explore other ways of representing the landscape where its subjective nature could remain rather more explicit. One of the most restrictive factors when talking about the landscape is the medium through which it is reproduced. Books and journals can only print small photographs and drawings (this article is a case

in point). The WWW, however, offers a significantly more flexible medium. The Web is not as restrained by the number of pages available, and it is possible to simultaneously include a whole variety of different interpretations and experiences of the landscape. We do not need to limit ourselves to academic styles of writing, and instead can experiment with alternative forms. Narratives written in the first, second, and third person can all help forge a bond between author and reader which is absent from normal passive texts (see Edmonds 1999). The inclusion of different accounts of the same landscape from a variety of different authors can also help to capture the multiplicity of meaning embedded in the landscape. I would also advocate the use of personal accounts and diary entries to help the reader understand the subjective experiences of the author. In addition, the WWW makes it possible to display many large colour images. All of these narrative forms can easily be reproduced on the WWW. This has already been done to a certain extent by the Bodmin Moor Project, whose WWW pages included a variety of narrative forms (see Table 1 for the URL).

With these approaches in mind I began to explore alternative ways of representing the landscapes of South Uist. Photography seemed to be an ideal means of rapidly and inexpensively capturing an impression of a landscape. The application of photography in archaeology has tended to be limited to site recording during excavation or fieldwork, rather than to communicate a sense of place (Shanks 1992). While individual photographic images are static, it is possible to combine multiple images to interesting effect (see Hockney 1984; Johnston in Bradley 1998b). It seems that there is considerable potential for photographs to be combined to create a greater sense of landscape.

4 QTVR—a methodology

In South Uist, 360 degree photographic montages were taken at each of the tombs visited. In each case a standard 35mm camera with a 35mm lens was used. Individual prints showing each sector of the horizon were captured by either turning around on the spot or by using a tripod to assist in the production of a level strip at a standard height above the ground. Unfortunately, any experimentation with cameras that pan around automatically, digital cameras or fish-eye lenses, was beyond the means of this project. Each panorama was taken in the forecourt area of each

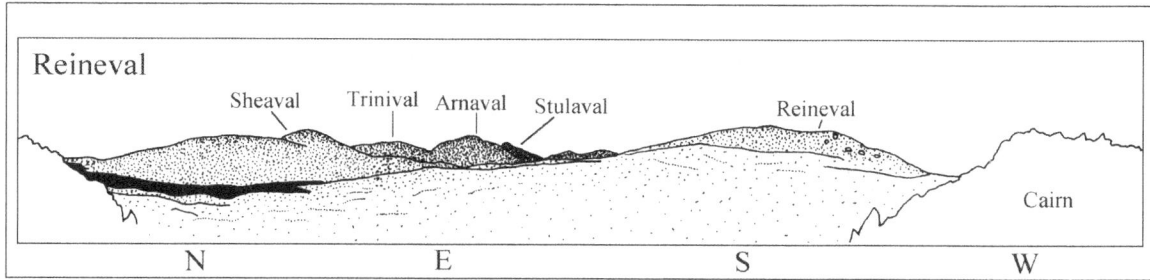

Figure 3: A 360 degree line-drawn panorama around the site of Reineval, standing in the forecourt.

tomb on the axis of the passage, where these architectural features could be identified. Each 360 degree photographic montage consisted of around nine standard 4×6 inch colour prints. The images were later joined together to form an extremely useful record which could be used in the interpretation of these sites once out of the field.

Although it is possible to manually paste the photographs together, they produce large photographic strips that are difficult to manage and impossible to include in any published format. Furthermore, such images can be viewed rapidly, which is quite unlike the experience of viewing a landscape, where the observer can only see in one direction at any one time. A more practical alternative was to scan each photograph and to recreate the montage on a computer. This method has many advantages including the ability to manipulate the image as well as convenient storage on disk or CD-ROM. In addition, such images can easily be displayed on the WWW.

Initial attempts to join together the scanned photographs using JASC Paintshop Pro version 4.15 (see Table 1 for the URL) produced mixed results. One of the main problems was that many of the photographs did not match up perfectly when stuck together, primarily due to distortion induced by camera optics. Another problem was balancing the exposure of each photograph, particularly the sky. This was primarily because an automatic camera with automatic exposure had been used. This problem can be greatly reduced by setting an exposure for the whole panorama manually. However, when the photographs are automatically exposed it produced a contrast between each photographic print that made the completed panorama appear disjointed. Blending the sky together convincingly using the 'Clone Brush' function on Paintshop Pro proved to be almost impossible. Image-stitching using this software was also time consuming, taking up to 6 hours to complete a single panorama. While each completed image required only one third of

a megabyte, and was thus ideal for presentation via the WWW, time constraints meant that alternative, faster methods of image-stitching were sought.

There are a number of software packages available on the market that are designed explicitly to smoothly stitch images together (Jayne Gidlow pers. comm.). The software package I eventually selected was SpinPanorama (see Table 1 for the URL), mainly because it was designed for PC and was available for use without licensing cost. The package is also straightforward to use. The scanned photographic prints are placed in the required sequence to complete the panorama. Next, two points are manually selected on each photo. These are the points which will be joined together (Figure 4). The software then automatically stitches the images together and blends the colours. The amount of time taken for this depends upon how well the images match one another, and the processing speed of the computer used. In these examples, each was completed in around half an hour. Although the results from this package were quite good, the image still needed to be refined using a graphics package. This is particularly necessary as SpinPanorama tends to leave black edges where it has had to bend the photographs together to match up properly (Figure 4). Once the image has been created and tidied-up, SpinPanorama converts the file into a continuous QTVR image which can be viewed using QuickTime plug-in software (see Table 1 for the URL). From start to finish, this method took approximately half an hour. One disadvantage over images produced using Paintshop Pro was that the final images exceeded a megabyte in size, which has implications for presentation on the WWW.

4.1 The results

Examples of digital photographic panoramas created using these techniques will be available on

17

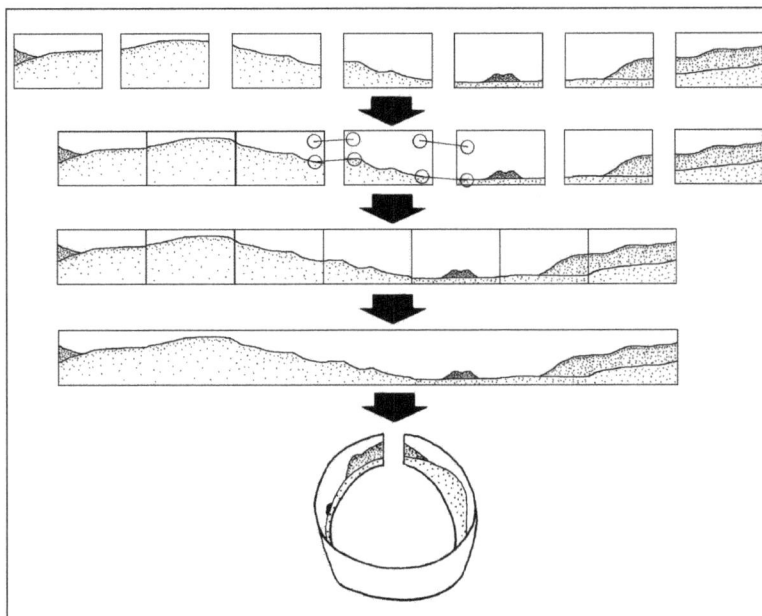

Figure 4: The process by which SpinPanorama pastes photographs together.

the WWW at http://www.intarch.ac.uk (Cummings 2000). The image of Reineval was created purely using SpinPanorama. This image has some blurred areas where the stitching has not worked effectively, but there are other advantages which compensate for these problems. Primarily, the montage is presented so that the reader can 'look' around the landscape from a fixed point, in this case standing in the façade of the cairn. The program is interactive, so that the user can control how they pan around the image in their own time. To some extent this reproduces the act of viewing a landscape, which is never visible in its totality. This overcomes the disadvantage of the complete strips which could be viewed in a single glance, and is rather less restricted than the narrow, static, photographs which can be reproduced on the printed page. A sense of looking is reintroduced, and motion returned to a two-dimensional image.

The chambered cairn of Barp Frobost was stitched together using Paintshop Pro. There is no blurring and the overall image is slightly sharper. This image also downloads rather more quickly. This is because it is about a quarter of the size of the file created using SpinPanorama. However, as outlined above, it is not always possible to stitch the photographs together with Paintshop Pro. While the final image can be clearer, it also far more time consuming to produce.

5   Critique

There are both advantages and disadvantages in creating QTVR images of the landscape. One major drawback is that the panoramas cannot reproduce the multisensual, and temporal impact of actually walking or moving around the landscape. While attempts are being made to allow the reader to gain a better sense of place by integrating sound, GIS, photographs, and video (see Mills this volume), their production remains at the experimental stage and is, at present, time consuming and sophisticated. While the future of landscape presentation may ultimately lie with these approaches, the creation of simple photographic panoramas outlined in this paper may, in the meantime, provide additional means of communicating landscape to a wider audience. From a practical point of view, these panoramas can be rapidly and cost effectively produced using equipment which is widely available: a standard 35mm camera, a scanner, computer and relevant software. Access to a digital camera may make the process even simpler. Unlike the creation of complex GIS databases or virtual reality, these images can be assembled quickly. Furthermore, the images can easily be viewed by any interested parties who have access to the WWW.

The panoramas were certainly found to portray a rather better sense of the landscape than simple photographs or plans. They provide a facility for other people to view the landscape for themselves, and perhaps to create their own interpretations. By having access to these images, it is also possible to conduct landscape analysis away from the field. Comparing such images may also reveal broader trends in the topographic settings of monuments located in different parts of the country.

In addition, there is some potential to explore alternative ways of representing the multisensory, active and experienced landscape. While the panoramas may privilege vision, they are at least located at a place in the world that can be viewed by people. This is more realistic than the abstract, floating perspective of maps and plans. The other disadvantage of these panoramas—that the landscape appears to be passive, fixed and atemporal—may to some extent be overcome by presenting a series of views taken at the same site but at different times of the day or year. It may also be possible to include in these images people experiencing the landscape, and vegetation and weather changes.

It seems clear then, that the production of QTVR panoramas can assist landscape archaeology in two ways. Firstly, by including these images it helps the author illustrate their arguments and interpretations much more effectively. Secondly, it also allows the reader to experience and interpret the landscape themselves. This is something that has not been possible before with books and journals.

6   Conclusions

Until recently it has been difficult to discuss landscape issues across the academic community because the media for communicating visual imagery has traditionally been limited to the constraints of the two-dimensional, static, printed page. In this sense, our depiction of landscape has not much changed from the sixteenth century paintings from which the word was coined. While moving video imagery has had some application in research, it has not often been used as a means of communicating experience to a wider audience. Video films, while capturing some degree of temporality, suffer from the disadvantage of being pre-recorded, and thus losing the sense of spontaneity which is otherwise natural to the observer. It seems that the only way we can attempt to show the reader the subjective, temporal and experienced nature of the landscape is by utilising a whole range of different written and visual media. Now, rapid advances in computer technology have brought a new range

of possibilities, and landscape archaeology would benefit enormously from the publication of landscape projects on the WWW. This would enable a variety of different accounts to be combined, thus helping to demonstrate the multiplicity of experience and meaning embedded in the landscape. An important contribution to this would be the inclusion of colour images that may help the reader to share both the experience, and also the significance, of the landscape with the author. This may, in turn, allow us to construct our own experiences and thus our own interpretations. While the word 'landscape' may have originally been used to describe painted images, it seems that technology is now increasingly allowing us to put our views of the world back into motion.

7   Acknowledgements

This paper is based upon fieldwork conducted with Niall Sharples and Cole Henley in South Uist. I would particularly like to thank Caitlin Buck for her encouragement, and Aled Cooke and Geoff Boden for assisting me with QTVR. Thanks also to Steve Trick for assistance with the SpinPanorama software and to the referees for useful comments on this paper.

References

[1] Armit, I. 1996. *The archaeology of Skye and the Western Isles.* Edinburgh, Edinburgh University Press.

[2] Bender, B. 1992. Theorising landscapes and the preshistoric landscapes of Stonehenge. *Man*, 27:735–755.

[3] Bender, B. 1993a. Introduction: landscape—meaning and action. In B. Bender, (ed.), *Landscape: politics and perspectives*, pp. 1–17. Oxford. Berg.

[4] Bender, B., (ed.) 1993b. *Landscape: politics and perspectives.* Oxford, Berg.

[5] Bender, B. 1998. *Stonehenge: making space.* London, Berg.

[6] Bradley, R. 1998a. Ruined building, ruined stones: enclosures, tombs and natural places in the Neolithic of south-west England. *World Archaeology*, 30(1):13–22.

[7] Bradley, R. 1998b. *The significance of monuments.* London, Routledge.

[8] Chapman, J. 1997. Place as timemarks—the social construction of prehistoric landscapes in eastern Hungary. In G. Nash, (ed.), *Semiotics of landscape: archaeology of mind*, International Series 661, pp. 31–45. Oxford, BAR.

[9] Cummings, V. 2000. The world in a spin: recreating the Neolithic landscapes of South Uist. *Internet Archaeology 8*. http://www.intarch.ac.uk, Accessed: 16/02/00.

[10] Cummings, V., Henley, C. and Sharples, N. forthcoming. The chambered tombs of South Uist. In M. Parker Pearson, (ed.), *From the mountains to the machair: a history of survey on the Outer Hebrides*. Sheffield, Sheffield Academic Press.

[11] Curry, M. 1998. *Digital Places: living with Geographic Information Technologies*. London, Routledge.

[12] Darvill, T. 1997. Landscapes and the archaeologist. In K. Barker and T. Darvill, (eds.), *Making English Landscapes*, pp. 70–91. Oxford, Oxbow.

[13] Duncan, J. 1993. Sites of representation: place, time and the discourse of the other. In J. Duncan and D. Ley, (eds.), *Place/culture/representation*, pp. 39–56. London, Routlege.

[14] Edmonds, M. 1999. *Ancestral Geographies of the Neolithic: landscape, monuments and memory*. London, Routledge.

[15] Gillings, M. and Goodrick, G. 1996. Sensuous and reflexive GIS: exploring visualization and VRML. *Internet Archaeology*, 1(1). http://www.intarch.ac.uk/journal/issue1/, Accessed:16/02/00.

[16] Haraway, D. 1991. *Simians, cyborgs and women: the reinvention of nature*. London, Free Association.

[17] Henshall, A. 1972. *The chambered tombs of Scotland, volume 2*. Edinburgh, Edinburgh University Press.

[18] Hockney, D. 1984. *Cameraworks*. London, Thames and Hudson.

[19] Ingold, T. 1993. The temporality of the landscape. *World Archaeology*, 1(25):152–175.

[20] Johnson, R. 1998. The paradox of landscape. *European Journal of Archaeology*, 3(1):313–325.

[21] Karlsson, H. 1997. *Being and post-processual archaeological thinking*. Goteborg, Gotarc Serie C, Arkeolgiska Skrifter no. 15.

[22] Kirk, T. 1997. Towards a phenomenology of building: the Neolithic long mound at La Commune-Sèche, Colombiers-sur-Seulles, Normandy. In G. Nash, (ed.), *Semiotics of landscape: archaeology of mind*, International Series 661, pp. 59–70. Oxford, BAR.

[23] Mills, S. F. 2000. An approach for integrating multisensory data: the examples of Sesklo and the Teleorman valley. In *this volume*, Oxford. BAR.

[24] Nash, G., (ed.) 1997. *Semiotics of landscape: archaeology of mind*. International Series 661. Oxford, BAR.

[25] Richards, C. 1996. Henges and water: towards an elemental understanding of monumentality and landscape in late Neolithic Britain. *Journal of Material Culture*, 1(2):313–336.

[26] Rodaway, P. 1994. *Sensuous Geographies*. London, Routledge.

[27] Shanks, M. 1992. *Experiencing the past: on the character of archaeology*. London, Routledge.

[28] Thomas, J. 1993. The politics of vision and the archaeologies of landscape. In B. Bender, (ed.), *Landscape: politics and perspectives*, pp. 19–48. Oxford, Berg.

[29] Thomas, J. 1996. *Time, culture and identity: an interpretive archaeology*. London, Routledge.

[30] Tilley, C. 1994. *A phenomenology of landscape*. Oxford, Berg.

[31] Tilley, C. 1999. *Metaphor and material culture*. Oxford, Blackwell.

[32] Wainwright, A. 1960. *The southern fells: a pictorial guide to the Lakeland fells*. Kendal, Westmoreland Gazette.

BCal: the development of an interactive Internet application

G. N. James

School of History and Archaeology
Cardiff University, PO BOX 909
Cardiff CF1 3XU, United Kingdom
gary.james@bigfoot.com

1 Introduction to Bayesian radiocarbon calibration

For many years archaeologists have used radiocarbon dating to help interpret the chronologies of past human activity. The first step in such dating is for the archaeologist to submit samples to a radiocarbon dating laboratory for scientific analysis. As a result of such analyses, the laboratory returns radiocarbon determinations which are an estimate of the radiocarbon age of each sample in the form of a mean and a standard error. However, because the proportion of radioactive carbon in the earth's atmosphere has not remained constant over time, such estimates are not on the calendar scale. Thus, in order to be of real use in creating chronologies, the radiocarbon ages must be converted (via appropriate calibration curves) onto the calendar scale.

Until recently, such calibrations were undertaken one sample at a time via computer programs such as CALIB (Stuiver and Reimer 1986, 1993). However, within the last decade a framework has been developed that utilizes Bayesian statistics to aid in the calibration process (Buck *et al.* 1996, chapter 9). This framework allows multiple radiocarbon determinations to be calibrated simultaneously and for related relative chronological information (arising from archaeological stratigraphy) to be included in the calibration process. Put more formally: we combine, via a statistical model, the radiocarbon determinations, suitable calibration curves, and any available *a priori* chronological information. This approach can result in improved accuracy in the calibrated dates and also gives rise to calendar date information about events which relate to the problem under study, but for which we have no direct absolute dating evidence.

2 Software for Bayesian radiocarbon calibration

This section introduces BCal which is a general purpose, easy to use Bayesian radiocarbon calibration software package. Its central component is another software program called Mexcal. I will now describe Mexcal, why it is probably unsuitable for archaeologists to use on its own, and how it fits in with BCal.

2.1 Mexcal

Mexcal is software which performs Bayesian radiocarbon calibration using methodologies published in a range of learned journals over the last 5–10 years (Buck *et al.* 1991, 1992, 1994a, 1994b, 1994c, 1996; Buck and Litton 1995; Christen 1994a, 1994b; Litton and Buck 1996; and Zeidler *et al.* 1998). It is a piece of robust software, written in C++, designed primarily for UNIX machines. Mexcal takes as input a text file known as Mexcal code. Mexcal code is a textual description of the radiocarbon data, the calibration curve(s) to use, and a concise representation of any *a priori* chronological information. The software performs a Bayesian analysis of all the supplied information using Markov Chain Monte Carlo (MCMC) simulation techniques. The output from Mexcal consists of the raw MCMC simulation data.

MCMC simulation techniques are typically mathematically sophisticated and CPU intensive. Consequently, Mexcal requires high performance machines with large amounts of CPU power, RAM and storage space. Depending on the amount of radiocarbon data and the complexity of the *a priori* chronological information, a calibration can take from under an hour to several days to complete. It is therefore important that Mexcal runs under a secure and stable operating system such as UNIX.

2.2 Problems with Mexcal

Mexcal is very difficult to use and most archaeologists simply do not, at present, have the computing expertise needed to write Mexcal code which is similar in structure to a computer programming language. In fact, even experienced computer programmers would face some problems when writing Mexcal code because Mexcal's input checking is rather limited. Small typos can lead to bizarre application behaviour and program crashes. In addition to this, the raw MCMC output is very difficult for humans to interpret. Quite sophisticated post-processing of the data has to be conducted before any archaeological interpretations can be made.

The difficulties associated with using Mexcal, combined with the need for powerful computing resources do not make Mexcal a viable option for most archaeologists. A new approach gives them access to Bayesian radiocarbon calibration software.

2.3 Making such software widely available

The problems presented by Mexcal are solved by developing BCal, an interactive Internet application. BCal provides various easy-to-use tools that allow the user to define their calibration problems via the Internet. Mexcal code is then automatically generated by BCal and submitted to Mexcal for calibration on a powerful UNIX machine. On completion of the calibration, BCal performs the necessary post-processing on behalf of the user. The user may then access the results of the calibration, again, via the Internet. By taking this approach the power of a user's own computer is almost irrelevant, because the actual processing takes place on a dedicated, remote, machine.

3 Internet applications

BCal is an Internet application. Internet applications are computer programs that are accessed via the Internet using appropriate access software. In the case of BCal, the appropriate access software is a standard World-Wide-Web browser. Unlike traditional applications, such Internet ap-

plications do not run directly on the user's own computer, but on a remote server that sends information and requests to the user at their own machine. In the remainder of this section we discuss the advantages and disadvantages of Internet applications, particularly with regard to BCal, and their basic hardware and software requirements.

3.1 Advantages of Internet applications

- From the user's perspective, Internet applications are platform independent. This means that provided the user has suitable access software, the applications can be used on any type of computer or operating system, e.g. Microsoft Windows, MacOS and UNIX.

- To use many modern Internet applications users need only a standard Web browser installed on their own computer. BCal is an application of this type and as such no specialist software need be installed on client machines.

- A user can access an Internet application from an Internet-enabled computer anywhere in the world. BCal even allows users to securely store their calibration projects on the server machine. This gives a user full access to their calibrations from the office, home, or even a conference.

- Some Internet applications provide users with access to special computer resources such as specialist information, and, in the case of BCal, a powerful CPU and storage space.

- Distribution of and access to software is straightforward. Traditionally, software is distributed using media such as floppy disks or CD-ROMs. No such distribution is required for Internet applications. A user requires only the URL of the Web site. With BCal, for example, the service provider can make updates, bug fixes, and new features available immediately.

- A service provider can easily find out how many people are using the software, where they use it from, which parts are used more frequently, and so on. This information can be used to help improve the service.

- The provider can restrict the use of the software to certain groups of people. They can even charge a subscription fee for access, or charge a user based on their usage of the software.

3.2 Disadvantages of Internet applications

- The performance of the software is determined by uncontrollable factors such as the speed of the Internet and a user's Internet connection.

- Depending on the technology used, the software may only be able to offer limited interactivity. New and improved Internet technologies are evolving which should gradually reduce this problem.

- A server machine permanently connected to the Internet is needed and this can be costly. If the application is small, a server may be available for little or no cost. However, if the application is large, like BCal, a dedicated server may need to be purchased.

3.3 Hardware and software requirements

3.3.1 Server (host) requirements

The main requirement is a computer that is permanently connected to the Internet. This computer acts as the server machine. In academia this is not such a problem, since academic networks are usually permanently connected to the Internet. Adequate file space will be needed on this machine to store the software and any user data. Web server software is required to run on the server machine. This software is responsible for interacting with the user's Web browser. There may be some additional requirements depending on the nature of the application. For example, BCal requires a high performance CPU and a large amount of RAM for running calibrations.

3.3.2 Client (user) requirements

A computer that can connect to the Internet is required; this connection can be temporary such as when a modem and phone line are used. In addition users require suitable access software such as a Web browser. These are now readily available and often distributed free of charge.

4 The technology behind BCal

This section describes the Internet technology behind BCal. There are a variety of different technologies available to help create Internet applications. BCal uses the Java Webserver and Java Servlets. These are introduced, together with a brief description of the information flow between a user's Web browser, the Java Webserver and Java Servlets. This information flow is the basis of BCal and many other Internet applications.

4.1 The Java Webserver

BCal uses the Java Webserver which is a fairly recent advance in server-side Internet technology. The Java Webserver is like most other Web server software in that it is responsible for interacting with the user's Web browser via the Internet. However, what makes the Java Webserver different is that it allows Java Servlets to be 'plugged in'. A Java Servlet is a special computer program that creates Web pages to display on the user's Web browser as well as processing information sent from the user's Web browser. They are very similar in functionality to CGI (common gateway interface) programs—perhaps the most widely used technology. However, Java Servlets are considered to have lower system overheads than CGI programs. They are also more secure, since badly written CGI programs can easily allow hackers to gain unauthorized access to a server machine.

4.2 The flow of information between the Web browser and the BCal software

Figure 1 and the list below show the flow of information between a user's Web browser and the BCal software.

1. The user views a Web page, generated by BCal, using a Web browser. This page may ask the user for information, e.g. some radiocarbon data. The user supplies this information via forms present on the page and clicks the 'Submit' button. The information is then sent, via the Internet, to the Java Webserver. This is known as an HTTP (Hyper-Text Transfer Protocol) request.

2. On reception of the HTTP request the Java Webserver invokes the Java Servlet specified in the HTTP request.

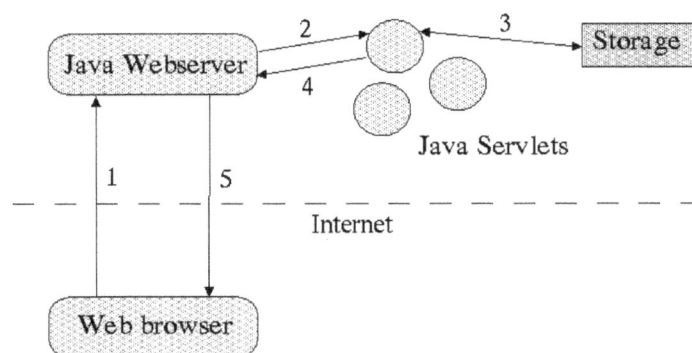

Figure 1: The flow of information between the user's Web browser and the BCal software.

3. The Java Servlet processes the information. This processing may involve some other action, such as storing or reading information within a file.

4. A new Web page is then created by the Java Servlet and passed to the Java Webserver. The content of this page is usually based on the information previously submitted and may ask the user for more information.

5. The Java Webserver will then send the newly composed page to the user's Web browser for viewing.

This cyclic flow continues throughout a user's session with BCal.

5 BCal software basics

This section provides a brief introduction to the software itself, starting with the basic requirements, followed by a description of the various tools contained within the software and the facilities they offer.

5.1 Accessing BCal

BCal can be accessed from almost any computer system, provided it has Internet access and a modern Web browser that supports 'frames' (e.g. Netscape 2+). In order to use BCal, a user must register themselves. Registering provides each user with their own personal BCal 'workspace', corresponding to secure file store on the BCal server machine. This workspace stores the user's projects, personal information, and configuration settings. A user gains access to the software and

their personal workspace by entering their user code and PIN, issued during the registration process, into a special page on the BCal Web site.

5.2 BCal's Web-based tools

BCal consists of four Web-based tools. These correspond to individual Java Servlets. Each of these tools is explained below.

5.2.1 Project manager

The project manager is the central tool of BCal. It is used to provide each user with the functionality they need to manage the projects within their BCal workspace. Such functions include creating and deleting workspace folders, moving projects between folders, and deleting them. The project manager is also used to access other parts of BCal. For example, the user may use the project manager to launch the definition editor to edit a particular project.

5.2.2 Definition editor

The definition editor is the most complex tool within BCal. It allows users to set up and define the *a priori* chronological information and radiocarbon data for projects. Figure 2 shows a screen shot of a typical page within the definition editor. The tool is designed to be as easy to use as possible. The user is asked questions about their calibration problem step-by-step until all the required information has been elicited. This elicitation process is split into several distinct stages. At any time the user may move back to previous stages to view or modify the information elicited. The tool performs validity

24

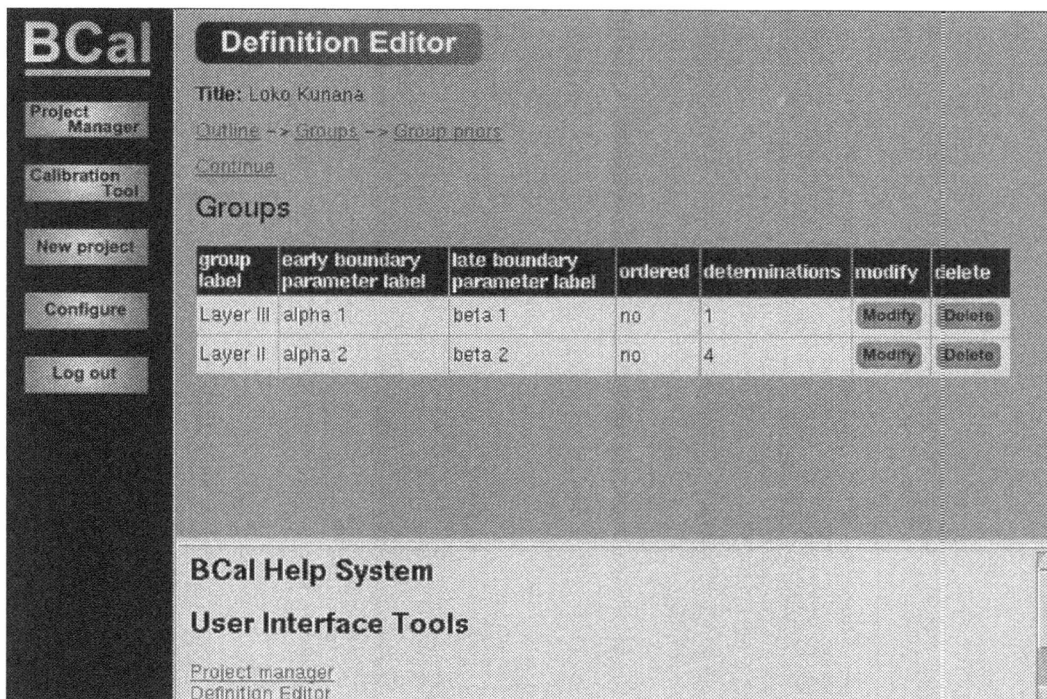

Figure 2: A screen shot of a typical page within the definition editor.

checks on all information entered, this includes checking the consistency of the supplied *a priori* chronological information.

Once the definition is complete, the user is provided with a graphical representation of the relative *a priori* chronological information, along with a tabular representation of any absolute *a priori* chronological information and radiocarbon data. Users are encouraged to compare BCal's interpretation of the calibration problem with their own perception and, if there are any discrepancies, the user may return to previous stages to make alterations.

5.2.3 Calibration tool

The calibration tool is responsible for initiating and controlling the Mexcal processes running on the BCal machine. When a project is submitted for calibration, Mexcal code is generated from the information supplied in the definition editor. Mexcal is then started with the generated Mexcal code.

Several independent Mexcal processes can run at once on the server machine, with the calibration tool monitoring the progress of them all. At any time, the user may view the progress of their calibrations and the others currently in progress on the same server. On completion of each calibra-

tion an e-mail message is sent to the user telling them that the results are available for viewing.

While Mexcal is running, the calibration tool also performs convergence checking on the raw MCMC data produced. Convergence checking is necessary to ensure that the results produced are mathematically reproducible. Unfortunately, it is widely accepted that it is impossible to reliably check convergence automatically; while BCal attempts to perform a limited amount of convergence checking, the user still needs to be aware of the strengths and weaknesses of MCMC simulation techniques, and it is essential that they conduct their own additional reliability tests. For example, to calibrate the project a few times on BCal to ensure the results obtained are sufficiently similar. In order to help users who have no experience in these matters, BCal provides a tutorial which includes an introduction to MCMC reliability and reproducibly issues, as well as an example of the steps required to undertake reliability tests.

5.2.4 Results presentation

The results presentation tool provides the user with the functionality they need to view and analyse the results of their calibrations. The user may view estimates of the calendar ages for events of interest, as well as estimates for the time elapsed between events of interest. These estimates may be viewed as posterior density plots and highest posterior density (HPD) regions. The format of the posterior density plots can be customized to suit each user's tastes and can easily be downloaded to their local machine in both scaleable and non-scaleable image files.

A probability analysis tool is also provided. This tool allows the user to define queries to determine the probability of certain scenarios being true, based on the calibrated results. An example of such a query may be to find the probability that the calendar date associated with a particular event is contained within the time interval spanned by a certain phase.

5.3 Availability

BCal was officially launched in Summer 1999 (Buck *et al.* 1999) and is available for use around the world. The service is free for non-commercial research purposes. To find out more, or to register for the service, visit the BCal home page at http://bcal.cf.ac.uk/. The home page contains an introduction to using the service and a detailed tutorial, as well as the software itself.

References

[1] Buck, C. E., Cavanagh, W. G. and Litton, C. D. 1996. *The Bayesian Approach to Interpreting Archaeological Data.* Chichester, Wiley.

[2] Buck, C. E., Christen, J. A. and James, G. N. 1999. Bcal: an online Bayesian radiocarbon calibration tool. *Internet Archaeology*, 7. http://intarch.ac.uk/journal/issue7/buck/, Accessed 17/02/00.

[3] Buck, C. E., Christen, J. A., Kenworthy, J. B. and Litton, C. D. 1994a. Estimating the duration of archaeological activity using C14 determinations. *Oxford Journal of Archaeology*, 13(2):229–240.

[4] Buck, C. E., Kenworthy, J. B., Litton, C. D. and Smith, A. F. M. 1991. Combining archaeological and radiocarbon information: a Bayesian approach to calibration. *Antiquity*, 65:808–821.

[5] Buck, C. E. and Litton, C. D. 1995. The radiocarbon chronology: further consideration of the Danebury dataset. In B. Cunliffe, (ed.), *Danebury: an Iron Age hillfort in Hampshire, Volume 6, A hillfort community in Hampshire*, pp. 130–136. London, Council for British Archaeology.

[6] Buck, C. E., Litton, C. D. and Scott, E. M. 1994b. Making the most of radiocarbon dating: some statistical considerations. *Antiquity*, 68:252–263.

[7] Buck, C. E., Litton, C. D. and Shennan, S. J. 1994c. A case study in combining radiocarbon and archaeological information: the early Bronze Age settlement of St. Veit-Klinglberg, Land Salzburg, Austria. *Germania*, 72:427–447.

[8] Buck, C. E., Litton, C. D. and Smith, A. F. M. 1992. Calibration of radiocarbon results pertaining to related archaeological events. *Journal of Archaeological Science*, 19:497–512.

[9] Christen, J. A. 1994a. *Bayesian interpretation of C14 results.* PhD thesis, University of Nottingham, Nottingham, UK.

[10] Christen, J. A. 1994b. Summarizing a set of radiocarbon determinations: a robust approach. *Applied Statistics*, 43(3):489–503.

[11] Litton, C. D. and Buck, C. E. 1996. An archaeological example: radiocarbon dating. In W. Gilks, S. Richardson and D. Spiegelhalter, (eds.), *Markov Chain Monte Carlo in Practice*, pp. 465–480. London, Chapman and Hall.

[12] Stuiver, M. and Reimer, P. J. 1986. A computer program for radiocarbon age calculation. *Radiocarbon*, 28(2B):1022–1030.

[13] Stuiver, M. and Reimer, P. J. 1993. Extended 14C database and revised CALIB radiocarbon calibration program. *Radiocarbon*, 35:215–230.

[14] Zeidler, J. A., Buck, C. E. and Litton, C. D. 1998. The integration of archaeological phase information and radiocarbon results from the Jama River Valley, Ecuador: a Bayesian approach. *Latin American Antiquity*, 9(2):160–179.

An approach for integrating multisensory data in archaeology: the examples of Sesklo and the Teleorman Valley

Steve Mills

School of History and Archaeology
Cardiff University, PO Box 909
Cardiff CF1 3XU, United Kingdom
email: MillsSF@Cardiff.ac.uk

1 Introduction

In this paper I highlight the advantages of using computers for developing a multisensory approach in archaeology; it will be argued that computer based techniques provide a valuable set of resources with which to articulate new ideas in ways which might not otherwise be possible. I have found that thinking with computers in a reflexive manner alongside theory and methodology has enabled me to further develop the research that I am presently conducting for a PhD. To elucidate these points I will first introduce the archaeological period and region my research concentrates on, then I present my reasons for developing a multisensory approach. I go on to discuss my methodology and use of computers. I finish by suggesting how my approach could prove beneficial for archaeological interpretation and its potential to make archaeological data accessible to wider audiences.

2 Research interests

The aim of the research is to extend our knowledge of Neolithic life (6500–3300 BC) in southeast Europe and particularly our understanding of tells (Figure 1). Tells represent the superimposition of repeated phases of the construction, use, abandonment and destruction of architecture over a delimited area. Over the course of several centuries, and in some cases millennia, these repeated phases of activity resulted in the formation of mounds. The volume of research and body of literature concerning tells is vast (for example Gimbutas *et al.* 1989; Renfrew *et al.* 1986; Todorova *et al.* 1983). The archaeology has been variously approached but the physical presence of tells has by and large taken precedent. Most research has assumed that concentrated complexes of architecture coupled with extensive floral and faunal deposits represents a sedentary Neolithic with tells considered almost as a by-product of the subsistence-economy. The landscape context of tells is inadequately studied and all too often reduced to little more than an economic resource base.

Recent research considers tells and their landscape contexts as on-going transformations of place, providing a variable setting for the social activities which permeated the everyday lives of Neolithic people (Bailey 1997). Regarding tells as 'living entities' (Bailey 1990) transforms them into phenomena which were historically and socially experienced; no longer are they reducible to sterile platforms upon which people acted, they become the necessary media for meaningful social action (Tringham 1991). To understand the appeal and enduring nature of tells and their landscape contexts, it must be recognised that *both* contributed to the experiences of Neolithic people and that these experiences were the foundation for a particular way of being in the world. Any research which acknowledges and substantiates this premise would do great justice to Neolithic ways of life. It is in the context of these recent research strategies that my research is being conducted.

The aim is to provide a multisensory approach for defining and interpreting archaeological contexts, expanding the current criteria for conceptualising and understanding the Neolithic in southeast Europe. Such an approach has made valuable recent contributions in other disciplines including anthropology (Feld 1996; Feld and Basso 1996; Stoller 1989; 1997), geography (Pocock 1989; 1993; Porteous 1985; 1986; Rodaway 1994)

Figure 1: Tell Măgura in the Claniţa river valley, southern Romania.

and music (Schafer 1969; 1973; 1977). These approaches have been successful by acknowledging the different ways in which cultures employ or define the senses.

Recent advances in vision and sound research within prehistoric monuments and landscapes in north-west Europe have been highly informative and have stimulated much discussion (Bradley 1993; Tilley 1994; Richards 1992; Watson and Keating 1999). This type of research needs to be extended to include south-east Europe. I aim to demonstrate that a deeper understanding can be achieved through an approach which considers concomitant visual and acoustic experiences as this will acknowledge that both are integral to the significance of place.

The research focuses on two areas of Neolithic south-east Europe with very different physical environments but with similar cultural material; south-east Thessaly in Greece and the Teleorman Valley in south-west Romania (Figure 2). Previously, cultural material in Romania has been explained along similar lines to material found further south in Greece and this has been largely irrespective of differences in the physical environment. Variation between tells is recognised based on differences between chronological sequences, physical dimensions, spatial configurations, material culture patterning and the presence and distribution of floral and faunal remains. However, it remains the case that the landscape context of tells has been inadequately studied.

I have conducted independent fieldwork at the site of Sesklo in Thessaly and as part of a joint Cardiff University-National Historical Museum of Romania project, the Southern Romania Archaeological Project (SRAP), in the Teleorman Valley. The tell at Sesklo dates from the Early Neolithic (around 6700 BC), tell Măgura in the Claniţa river valley, southern Romania, dates from the Late Neolithic (around 4500 BC). Alongside this chronological difference there are differences in the type, range and quantity of both cultural material and floral and faunal remains present. These differences are recognised in traditional studies, I am suggesting that the variation is greater still. There is a striking contrast in the physical environment between the two areas and this significantly influences associated visual and acoustic experiences (Figures 3 and 4). I advance the possibility that differences in the surrounding landscapes in the two areas gave rise to different ranges of sensory stimuli in prehistory and thus to different lived experiences associated with the tells. This leads on to the subject of recent landscape studies.

3 Landscape, phenomenology and the senses

The definition and use of the term landscape has been the focus of much recent discussion and I do not wish to elaborate on those themes here. For the purposes of this paper, landscape is taken to mean all those elements of the physical environment which both surround and with which an individual/community interacts. This includes the perceptual frameworks through which that environment is understood in terms of cultural, natural, economic and his-

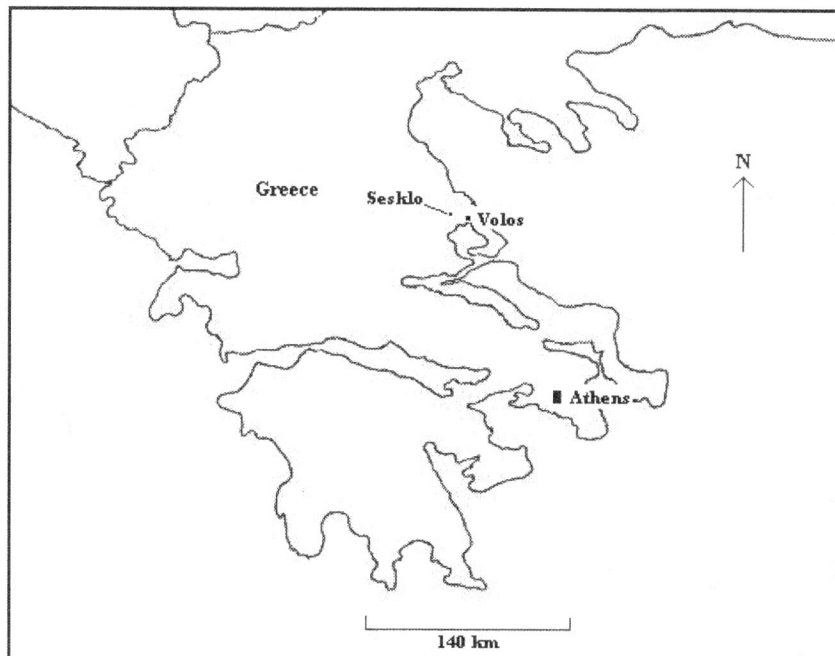

(a) Map of Greece showing Sesklo in south-east Thessaly.

(b) Map of Romania showing the area of the Teleorman Valley.

Figure 2: The research areas in Greece (a) and Romania (b).

Figure 3: The physical environment at Sesklo, Thessaly.

Figure 4: The physical environment in the Teleorman Valley.

toric relations. Landscape studies have featured prominently in recent research and publications, many of which have adopted phenomenological approaches (Tilley 1994; Thomas 1996). I have been inspired by these works but I wish to make a few points clear as regards my own position relative to these.

The aim of phenomenology is to provide a universally applicable interpretation of the intentional and practical actions of humans in their surroundings (Brück 1998). The human body is central—as individuals move, the world is experienced from particular perspectives. Placement, orientation and movement at and between locales help structure interpretation. A strong theme of post-modernism is that the body is a social construct, it is culturally specific and different people have different social identities. If the human body mediates experience then different concepts of the body are likely to place differential emphasis on the senses. However, the phenomenologies applied in recent archaeological studies have been dominated by a marked visualism, which, it can be argued, reflects Western twentieth century perspectives. Visualism represents a way of exploring and recording which favours seeing and visual tools, it further implies a visual conditioning by which problems are conceptualised and thought about (Rodaway 1994, 116).

Visibility studies provide valuable contributions and produce stimulating results, the point I wish to make here is that we can go further. By drawing attention to the contemporary primacy of vision it becomes evident that there is an imbalance in research; non-visual forms of data have often been neglected. This situation needs to be reformulated. By stating this I am not suggesting that our visual primacy is problematic in itself, rather that we, as archaeologists, need to be more explicit about its role in the production of knowledge.

It should be recognised that our sensory experiences of a landscape are likely to differ from those of Neolithic people. This premise should be our point of departure. My concern is not with precisely defining the nature of Neolithic sensoriums but to acknowledge that they played a significant role. I propose that it is possible to investigate the mechanisms of sensory experiences in the present and to use this to begin to think about how those mechanisms may have operated in the past. The process should begin by investigating how the archaeological record forms part of the constitution of contemporary societies by way of sensory experiences.

For a given context, a multisensory approach would consider all the senses simultaneously and on an equal basis, thereby challenging the implicit visualism of many accounts. Ideally my research would follow this path but given the logistical constraints imposed by a finite research period, I have restricted my research to the study of vision and sound. I have chosen vision and sound because they are the senses with which I am most familiar, in terms of the physical and physiological processes involved, and because they lend themselves more readily to quantification and representation. I must point out that the methodology I employ makes great use of visual techniques which some may consider contradictory to my earlier comments. I recognise the irony in using an almost exclusively visual media (the computer) to challenge claims of visualism and to stress the multisensory nature of experience. I advocate that this irony needs to be embraced and treated as a significant point of departure. By concentrating on the senses we can effectively engage with a computer (vision and sound), we can develop the means to study the other senses. This brings me to my methodology and use of computers.

4 Fieldwork methodologies and computing

The integrated and variable nature of the senses requires that a range of techniques be adopted to record, manipulate, present and interpret audio-visual data. Recent advances in information technology and multimedia provide archaeologists with new opportunities to articulate their ideas. This is my rationale for using computing; a multisensory approach will be best achieved using available multimedia technology.

It is appropriate to investigate the senses in a combined and systematic manner. To achieve this, part of the research involves creating a computer-based integrator capable of combining spatial, visual and acoustic data sets. I am using a GIS as a platform for integrating photographic, sound recording and virtual reality data sets. The system is based around Microsoft Windows 95 (see Table 1 for the URL) running Environmental Systems Research Institute's ArcInfo and ArcView software (ESRI 1990). The GIS software enables existing spatial data-sets and audio-visual data collected during fieldwork to be combined in a relational manner, geo-referenced within the same co-ordinate system and accessed at the same time. The GIS will be structured

Web Site	URL	Accessed
Apple QuickTime	http://quicktime.apple.com	15/02/00
Microsoft	http://www.microsoft.com	16/02/00
PictureWorks	http://www.pictureworks.com	14/03/00

Table 1: Associated Web sites of software cited in the text.

in such a way as to allow specified locations on a digitised topographical map to be selected and to access the audio-visual data relevant to that location. The applications I employ will be familiar to those who use computers and GIS. The novelty of the approach lies in its ability to integrate and make accessible a range of data sets within the same environment. This removes the need to flick between maps, archaeological publications (containing field walking, surface collection and excavation data) and image and sound computer files.

Two separate projects have been created using ArcView; one for Sesklo and one for the Teleorman Valley. Both projects are structured with a number of levels with each level containing particular types of data sets. Each level corresponds to a view or scene in the ArcView projects. A general description of each level is given below.

4.1 Level One: topographic maps and archaeological data

I am creating the spatial database using ArcInfo to digitise the topographical map and site plans of Sesklo; the topographical map of the Teleorman Valley and additional archaeological data obtained during the SRAP 1998/9 seasons. All data sets in the GIS will be geo-referenced. In the case of Sesklo this will be achieved by reference to the site plan and map co-ordinates. In the case of the Teleorman Valley this will be achieved by reference to the ground survey grid system established during fieldwork.

I am aware of recent discussions and critiques regarding the use of GIS in archaeology, particularly with respect to the abstractions involved in reducing three-dimensional space into two-dimensional map-like data. Whilst accepting these issues, I also recognise the value of maps for the role they play in constituting part of our contemporary understanding of the geographic world: maps are a useful media for representing spatial distributions and relationships. In this study the GIS is being used to integrate map data with audio-visual data rather than to conduct advanced spatial analysis.

The audio-visual data will be collected during fieldwork at Sesklo and in the Teleorman Valley. This will be achieved using photography and sound recording and measuring equipment.

4.2 Level Two: visual data

The rationale for using photography is to collect panoramic images that reflect static visual relationships between sites and the surrounding landscape. This procedure follows and improves upon my previous work at Sesklo during which significant visual relationships between the spatial organisation of the site and surrounding natural features were identified (Mills 1997). Specific locations at the sites and in the landscape will be selected from which panoramic mosaics of photographs will be taken. These locations will be referenced using map and grid co-ordinates. The panoramic mosaics will reflect, in the first instance, what can be seen of the surrounding landscape from any given site and in the second, from where such a site can be seen from the surrounding landscape.

After the fieldwork the photographs will be scanned and stitched together into 120-degree views (limit of human visibility) using software such as PictureWorks' SpinPanorama (see Cummings this volume, see Table 1 for the URL). I will then embed the panoramas in the GIS. 'Hotlinks' will bring up panoramas relevant to selected locations along with explanatory text documenting orientation and feature information (Figure 5).

4.3 Level Three: acoustic data

The rationale for using sound recording and measurement is to collect data on the local acoustic properties at Sesklo and in the Teleorman Valley and from Romanian farmsteads in the same valley. Acoustic data on the ambient sound environment at sites, farmsteads and in the landscape will be recorded and measured. The sound recordings and measurements will be referenced using map and grid survey co-ordinates (the location of sound recording stations will necessarily

(a) View from Sesklo A towards Sesklo B.

(b) View from Sesklo B towards Sesklo A.

Figure 5: View from Sesklo A towards Sesklo B (a) and the opposite view from Sesklo B to Sesklo A (b)

take into consideration the presence of modern human-made sounds). This procedure will capture data on local sounds such as rivers and wild and domesticated animals. The recorded audio data will be converted into Windows 'wave' files and accessed from the GIS via hotlinks to a suitable media-player. Decibel measurements (taken using a sound-level meter) will be represented in graph form and embedded in the GIS. It will also be of interest to produce spectrograms of ambient sounds reflecting their inherent frequency distributions. This can be achieved by combining soundcard and spectrogram software. If the two study areas have different wild and domesticated species then it is likely that this will result in different ambient soundscapes. The resulting spectrogram images will be embedded in the GIS. Figure 6 provides example spectrograms, one of the sound of a cow lowing and one of the sound of a sheep baaing.

4.4 Level Four: virtual data

It will be apparent by now that the data sets to be incorporated within the GIS will reflect the sites and their surrounding landscapes as they appear visually and acoustically in the present. Now, if I were to follow the traditional phenomenological approach then such data would be sufficient material on which to base interpretations of audio-visual experiences in the Neolithic. However, the data integrator should be considered as providing a point of departure for archaeological investigation; it is an exploratory tool for investigating contemporary experiences. Only after this understanding has been reached can we begin to consider how things might have been otherwise.

Virtual reality can be used to model how landscapes may have influenced Neolithic audio-visual experiences. Advances in visual and acoustic rendering certainly allow for this possibility. The purpose of such virtual reality models would be to identify those components of the physical and built environments that have been lost between the Neolithic and the present and to put those components back into the equation as far as is possible. It is unlikely that the evidence will ever be sufficient to produce accurate reconstructions of the past, any virtual construct should be considered as an aid to conceptualisation rather than as an attempt to achieve realism. It is possible to generate simple virtual scenes within ArcView using the 3D Analyst extension. By comparing virtual (Neolithic) datasets and present day data-sets it will be possible to identify potential differences in the range of variables that contribute to audio-visual experiences. I suggest that this procedure would provide a more secure basis for interpretation. Currently 3D virtual scenes of the two study areas are being produced. The 3D virtual scenes will be given textures reflecting, in a very general way, how the landscapes may have appeared in the Neolithic. I will then compare and contrast the various datasets and use the results so gathered as the basis for my interpretations.

5   Future Research

Further proposed research by the author will employ video. The rationale for using video would be to record real-time audio-visual data from the perspective of a mobile human subject at and around sites and in the landscape. This would be of value for understanding the relationships between the physical and built environments, sensory experiences and bodily movements. Video data could be captured in walks across areas of archaeological significance and referenced using map and grid survey co-ordinates. The video data could then be transferred into computer format using a video capture device. The resulting Apple QuickTime movies (see Table 1 for the URL) could again be accessed from the GIS via geo-referenced hotlinks indicating where the video footage was recorded.

Future research could take the application of virtual constructs further still. The concepts of stitch-panoramas and video walk-throughs represent methodologies that can be used equally effectively in virtual worlds. This would provide a stronger link to the methodologies advanced above for the study of modern contexts. The same could apply to virtual soundscapes produced on the basis of material culture patterning and faunal and floral remains. Such virtual constructs would provide new ways of thinking about the past.

I advance the data integrator as an innovative tool which can further our understanding of the Neolithic in southeast Europe. It is able to do this by virtue of the relational manner in which a range of different data sets are combined. This encourages archaeologists to be more explicit about their own experiences in particular contexts in the present thereby providing a more secure foundation for thinking about how those contexts may have been experienced differently in the past.

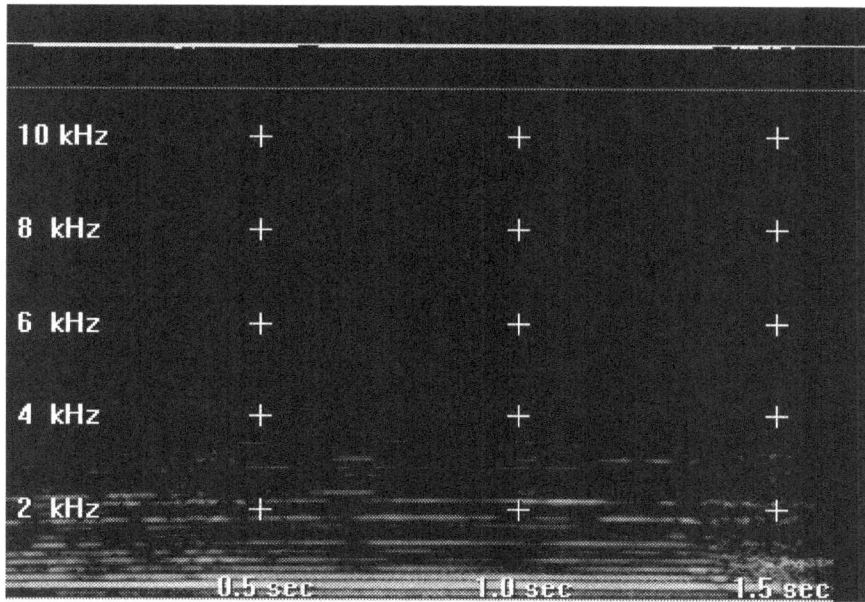

(a) Spectrogram of a cow.

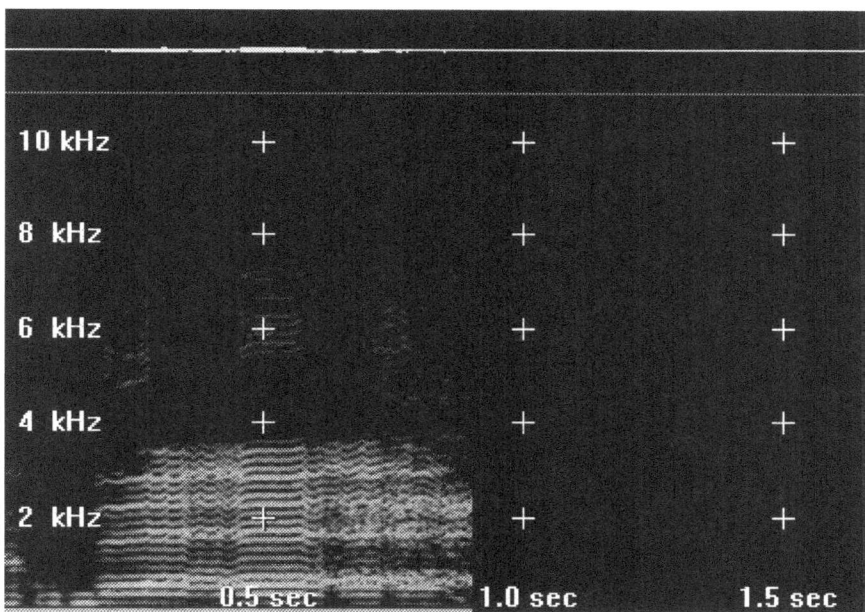

(b) Spectrogram of a sheep.

Figure 6: Spectrogram images embedded in the GIS.

6 Conclusions

I began the PhD with the idea of studying concomitant visual and acoustic experiences (I had a theory and a field methodology) but I had no idea how to bring the data together in a meaningful way. Computer applications have provided a solution to this problem, these have had repercussions on the fieldwork methodology I employ and have encouraged me to refine my original theoretical position and to consider how I can take the process further. I hope to have shown how my use of computers is closely linked with the theory and methodology I am employing, I would like to think that this constitutes good archaeological practice. As computing becomes more mainstream in archaeology it is imperative that their application maintains a healthy and reciprocal relationship with theory and methodology.

The multisensory approach I advance, its methodology and its use of computing I consider to be a useful contribution to archaeology. The approach is still in the developmental stage and many solutions have yet to be found, I therefore welcome any comments and criticisms. As I see it, a multisensory approach is as much a concern with thinking about ourselves, our preconceptions and archaeological practice in general as it is a concern with identifying the constitutions of past social realities. Having said that, it is hoped that an attentiveness to the former will lead to new understandings of the latter. Further to this, it is my hope that through the use of computing, academic archaeology will become increasingly accessible to wider audiences. Looking to the future, I think it would be of value to install a facility, something like the one outlined above, in the public domain, which is structured in such a way as to allow feedback. This would enable a wide variety of people from different social backgrounds (ethnic identity, age, gender, status, physical abilities) to provide valuable information reflecting the variability of human experiences in relation to archaeological sites and their environs. Such accessibility and feedback can only lead to more informed archaeologies.

7 Acknowledgements

I would like to thank the following for their support and comments during the production and presentation of this paper: Dr. Douglass Bailey, Dr. Caitlin Buck, Mr. Cole Henley, Mr. Aled Cooke, Dr. Paul Pan and Mr. Steve Trick.

References

[1] Bailey, D. W. 1990. The living house: signifying continuity. In R. Samson, (ed.), *The social archaeology of houses*, pp. 19–48. Edinburgh, Edinburgh University Press.

[2] Bailey, D. W. 1997. Villages of silence: cemeteries of sound. Paper presented at the Archaeology of the Voice Conference, Aberystwyth April 1997.

[3] Bradley, R. 1993. *Altering the earth: the origins of monuments in Britain and Continental Europe*. Edinburgh, Society of Antiquaries of Scotland (Monograph series number 8).

[4] Brück, J. 1998. In the footsteps of the ancestors: a review of Tilley's 'A phenomenology of landscape: places, paths and monuments. *Archaeological Review from Cambridge*, 15(1):23–36.

[5] ESRI 1990. *Understanding GIS: the ARC/INFO method*. Environmental Systems Research Institute, California.

[6] Feld, S. 1996. Waterfalls of song: an acoustemology of place resounding in Bosavi, Papua New Guinea. In S. Feld and K. H. Basso, (eds.), *Senses of place*, pp. 91–135. Santa Fe, New Mexico, School of American Research Press.

[7] Feld, S. and Basso, K. H., (eds.) 1996. *Senses of place*. Santa Fe, New Mexico, School of American Research Press.

[8] Gimbutas, M., Winn, S. and Shimabuku, D. 1989. *Achilleion: a Neolithic settlement in Thessaly, Greece, 6400–5600 BC*. Los Angeles, University of California, Institute of Archaeology.

[9] Mills, S. F. 1997. Towards a systematic approach to the study of visual experiences in prehistory: investigations at Neolithic Sesklo. Master's thesis, Cardiff University.

[10] Pocock, D. C. D. 1989. Sound and the geographer. *Geography*, 74:193–200.

[11] Pocock, D. C. D. 1993. The senses in focus. *Area*, 25(1):11–16.

[12] Porteous, J. D. 1985. Smellscape. *Progress in Human Geography*, 9(3):356–378.

[13] Porteous, J. D. 1986. Intimate sensing. *Area*, 18(3):250–251.

[14] Renfrew, A. C., Gimbutas, M. and Elster, E. S. 1986. *Excavations at Sitagroi: a prehistoric village in northeast Greece.* Los Angeles, University of California.

[15] Richards, C. 1992. Doorways into another world: the Orkney-Cromarty chambered tombs. In N. Sharples and A. Sheridan, (eds.), *Vessels for the ancestors*, pp. 62–76. Edinburgh, Edinburgh University Press.

[16] Rodaway, P. 1994. *Sensuous geographies.* London, Routledge.

[17] Schafer, R. M. 1969. *The new soundscape.* Scarborough, Ontario, Berandol Music Limited.

[18] Schafer, R. M. 1973. *The music of the environment.* Wien, Universal Edition A.G.

[19] Schafer, R. M. 1977. *The tuning of the world.* New York, Alfred A. Knopf.

[20] Stoller, P. 1989. *The taste of ethnographic things: the senses in anthropology.* Philadelphia, University of Pennsylvania Press.

[21] Stoller, P. 1997. *Sensuous Scholarship.* Philadelphia, University of Pennsylvania Press.

[22] Thomas, J. 1996. *Time, culture and identity.* London, Routledge.

[23] Tilley, C. 1994. *A phenomenology of landscape: places, paths and monuments.* Oxford, Berg.

[24] Todorova, H., Vasilev, V., Ianusevich, Z., Kovacheva, M. and Vulev, P., (eds.) 1983. *Ovcharovo.* Razkopki i Prouchvaniya 8. Sofia, Bulgarian Academy of Sciences, Institute of Archaeology.

[25] Tringham, R. 1991. Households with faces: the challenge of gender in prehistoric architectural remains. In J. Gero and M. Conkey, (eds.), *Engendering archaeology: women and prehistory*, pp. 93–131. Oxford, Blackwell.

[26] Watson, A. and Keating, D. 1999. Architecture and sound: an acoustic analysis of megalithic monuments in prehistoric Britain. *Antiquity*, 73:325–326.

Developing an archaeology soapbox and marketplace on the WWW

Leonel Morgado and Mila Simões de Abreu

GeIRA Project

University of Trás-os-Montes e Alto Douro - Computer Centre

Quinta de Prados, 5000 Vila Real, Portugal

email: leonelm@utad.pt, msabreu@utad.pt

1 Introduction

Although the World-Wide-Web (WWW) is probably one of the most powerful and successful media for scientific publishing, brainstorming and communication existing today, finding relevant material about special interest areas like archaeology or rock-art can be frustrating. A search for 'archaeology' on WWW indexes like Yahoo (please see Table 1 for the Yahoo URL, and for all other WWW sites mentioned in the text below) often generates dozens of links and when one browses apparently pertinent categories, it is common to find themes like 'Books', and 'Companies' listed side by side with 'Mummification' and 'Folsom Points'!

Special interest WWW sites could benefit greatly from appropriate expertise, as 'About.com' and other locations prove; however, many experts may not have the time and know-how to handle the specialised applications and programming required to put material on-line effectively. Intuitive resources and assistance should be available to make this possible. Initiatives like 'Rock Art Net' illustrate the advantages of navigational interfaces for potential contributors.

Our proposed hosting address or soapbox for archaeology and connected fields would have a WWW-server-based engine supporting the navigational and design requirements of researchers, so providing easily accessible space and media for publishing on the Internet. It would be enhanced by an index having various sections compiled and organised by experts in corresponding fields. A potentially throbbing marketplace of ideas—with discussion areas, mailing lists and other forms of interaction that are emerging—would go hand-in-hand with the soapbox.

2 Current status of WWW indexes and hosting sites

On 16th June 1999, a search for 'archaeology' on Yahoo yielded 80 'category matches', i.e. 80 assemblages of sites or further subdivisions, and 769 'sites', i.e. sites whose description or name included the word 'archaeology'. While the category matches include several specific themes, these were not derived from the 'Archaeology' theme itself but rather from the overall information structure of Yahoo—some of the themes just happen to have archaeology sites associated with them. This is reflected by the fact that, of the 80 category matches, only 11 were true category matches, the remaining 68 were actually regional matches (see Figure 1).

The 'Full Coverage' and 'Net Events' links direct us to Yahoo pages with news on these subjects. Useful as they may be, they are not the document repository or information pointer we desire. From the list in Figure 1, we see that the most general link is 'Social Science > Anthropology and Archaeology > Archaeology'. Following it, we get 25 links to sites with general information and a categorisation of the subject (see Figure 2).

The main problem with this listing is its classification: main themes such as 'Education', 'Companies' or 'Books' are listed alongside 'Folsom Points', 'Mummification' and 'Repatriation and Reburial Issues'. WWW indexes based on a human expert yield much better targeting; a search on About.com for 'archaeology' yields only one 'About.com Recommends' and 1,493 non-categorised sites. Going straight into that 'recommendation'—'Archaeology - Home Page', we get a page with some recent additions, sites 'In the Spotlight' and a categorisation of net

WWW resource	URL	Accessed
Yahoo	http://www.yahoo.com/	27/01/00
About.com	http://www.about.com/	27/01/00
Rock Art Net	http://www.rupestre.net/	27/01/00
ArchNet	http://archnet.uconn.edu/	27/01/00
ARGE	http://odur.let.rug.nl/~arge/	27/01/00
CBA	http://www.britarch.ac.uk/info/uklinks.html	27/01/00
BUBL	http://bubl.ac.uk/link/hum.html	27/01/00
Geocities	http://www.geocities.com/	27/01/00
Terràvista	http://www.terravista.pt/	27/01/00
Altavista	http://www.altavista.com/	27/01/00
HotBot	http://www.hotbot.com/	27/01/00
Museum of Abade de Baçal	http://www.utad.geira.pt/museus/abadebacal/	27/01/00
Museum of Moncorvo	http://www.utad.geira.pt/museus/ferromoncorvo/	27/01/00
Museum of Mogadouro	http://www.utad.geira.pt/museus/mogadouro/salamuseu/	27/01/00
IRAC '98 WWW site	http://www.utad.geira.ps/irac/	27/01/00

Table 1: URLs of WWW resources cited in the text.

Social Science > Anthropology and **Archaeology**
Full Coverage > Science > Anthropology and **Archaeology**
Social Science > Anthropology and **Archaeology** > **Archaeology**
Social Science > Anthropology and **Archaeology** > **Archaeology** > Marine **Archaeology**
Business and Economy > Companies > Scientific > Anthropology and **Archaeology**
Arts > Humanities > History > By Time Period > Ancient History > Roman Empire > **Archaeology**
Society and Culture > Cultures and Groups > Cultures > Mayan > **Archaeology**
Social Science > Anthropology and **Archaeology** > **Archaeology** > Biblical **Archaeology**
Social Science > Anthropology and **Archaeology** > **Archaeology** > Urban **Archaeology**
Business and Economy > Companies > Travel > Tour Operators > **Archaeology**
Net Events > Social Science > Anthropology and **Archaeology**

Figure 1: The true category matches from Yahoo.

links. We still find the same classification problem: 'Africa' is at the same level as 'Scandinavia', 'Computing' and 'Ceramics'. While these categorisations are more useful than those returned by Yahoo (because they are theme-oriented and not site-classification-oriented) the entire task is in the hands of one person. So far, no commercial site has employed the services of several experts for optimal classification of the secondary subjects. Fortunately, several non-commercial sites provide expert indexing archaeological resources on the WWW. These include the ArchNet, 'the WWW Virtual Library for Archaeology', but also ARGE, the Archaeological Resource Guide for Europe, the Council for British Archaeology (CBA) links, for British Archaeology, and the BUBL list of archaeological resources. The category list of ArchNet, in particular, has a really useful classification (see Figure 3).

These expert-driven indexes are much more useful, but for successful maintenance and updat-

ing of such a categorisation, several experts are required. ARGE, for instance, states: 'How do links end up in ARGE? ...we find out about these new pages, [produced by people, on their own], either because they then inform us of the URL directly, or because one of our correspondents has spotted the new URL (keep up the good work, you lot!), or because it turned up in the regular WWW searches conducted by ARGE'.

Thus we have a class of WWW indexes that (due to lack of human resources) have poor classification performances. Another class, does not fair much better in terms of updating, but is more useful, in that it provides human, expert-driven classification. Finally, we have sites like Rock Art Net, which present a classified index on a specific area, achieve much more detailed categorisation and accept articles for publication on-line.

Also available via the Internet, we have a vast number of organisations that host WWW sites for free, such as Geocities or Terràvista. This

- **Regions** *(24)*

- **Ancient Art**	- **Marine Archaeology** *(61)* NEW!
- **Archaeoastronomy** *(14)*	- **Megaliths** *(13)*
- **Archaeometry** *(10)*	- **Middle Ages** *(19)*
- **Biblical Archaeology** *(15)*	- **Mummification** *(6)*
- **Books**	- **Museums and Exhibits** *(43)*
- **Companies**	- **Organizations** *(39)*
- **Education** *(1)*	- **Prehistoric** *(27)*
- **Egyptology**	- **Remote Sensing** *(7)*
- **Events** *(5)*	- **Repatriation and Reburial Issues**
- **Fieldwork and Expeditions** *(46)*	- **Rock Art** *(36)*
- **Folsom Points** *(6)*	- **Tour Operators**
- **Institutes** *(54)*	- **Urban Archaeology** *(11)*
- **Journals** *(22)*	- **Web Directories** *(12)*
- **Magazines** *(5)*	- **Zooarchaeology** *(7)*

Figure 2: Links to sites with general information.

can be seen simply by searching Yahoo for 'Free WWW Hosting'. On the 16th of June, 1999, we got 5 category matches and 242 site matches. By allowing the users to create WWW sites, one's efforts can be used to promote a site, a theme, study area, whatever. But not many archaeologists are skilled in WWW site construction and management. Even if they were, some graphic design skills are also required if we want people to really stop at the site and read or gaze at its contents. Graphic appeal is the key to making a site effective (McGovern 1999).

3   The search engine perspective and the importance of metadata

Another way to find more relevant information might be to improve the accuracy of search engines such as Altavista, HotBot and others. This is in fact a very important issue, but the service that search engines provide is quite distinct from that of WWW indexes. The former provide bulk information that the user must wade through and evaluate; the latter provide categorised information, not so vast in scope, but much more time-efficient regarding retrieval of useful information.

Our primary focus is on sites that provide this latter kind of service: indexing. One aspect of search engines is, however, of some interest and worth mentioning here. That is the usage of metadata. Metadata, meaning 'data about data', provides a way to describe a document's content,

allowing search engines to better associate the document with specific keywords.

Our concept, discussed below, can be summed up as 'the mixing of indexers with hosting sites', i.e., creating a site that is not only an index but also a place to host sites, with simple but efficient layout tools. Since the concept includes site-creation tools, those tools should incorporate metadata into the sites, to improve their visibility outside the indexer itself.

Weibel *et al.* (1995), stated that 'a reasonable alternative way to obtain usable metadata for electronic resources is to give authors and information providers a means to describe the resources themselves, without having to undergo the extensive training required to create records conforming to established standards'. It is not this paper's purpose to discuss the archaeological applications of metadata, further than to register its importance as a link to the overall Internet community. Metadata tags are important since Internet users frequently comes across sites only by using search engines.

For the reader who wishes to delve into this subject, we recommend the paper by Weibel *et al.* (1995), which includes a description of the set of metadata elements known as the Dublin Core, and also the draft paper by Miller (1996), about an application of the Dublin Core.

Academic Departments
Archaeological Regions
    Africa
    Asia
    Australia and Pacific
    Central America
    Europe
    Near East
    North America
    South America
Featured Site
Museums on the Web
News & System Information
Other Resources
    Email Directory (WEDA)
    Electronic Journals
    Newsgroups & Listservs
    Publishers

Search ArchNet
Subject Areas
    Archaeometry
    Botanical
    Ceramics
    CRM & Government
    Agencies
    Educational Materials
    Ethnohistory /
    Ethnoarchaeology
    Faunal
    Geo-Archaeology
    Historic Archaeology
    Lithics
    Mapping and GIS
    Method & Theory
    Site Files & Tours
    Software
HELP

Figure 3: The category list on ArchNet.

4 Our concept

We propose a site that would act as a useful, specialised index for archaeology while offering archaeologists the possibility of having their sites hosted for free and with a certain amount of graphic design in order to make sure they are at least minimally appealing. This follows on from a basic concept outlined by van Leusen *et al.* (1996) who proposed a 'service building on and extending the ways archaeological information is accessed by ArchNet and ArchWEB-NL'. This would be complemented by 'establishing one or more servers either dedicated entirely to archaeology or piggybacking on existing servers'.

The number of servers dedicated to our proposed site is not relevant to the idea itself, since there are several purely technical solutions to the scalability problem, which are beyond the scope of this paper. Our proposed 'site' could be an entirely new site; it could also be an enhancement or companion to an already existing site whose author possesses the classification expertise required. It expands on van Leusen *et al.*'s (1996) idea by proposing the distribution of the development and updating of the categorisation, as well as providing a remote method for creation of graphically appealing pages. The key ideas or 'rules' behind it are:

- Site categorisation operates only at the top level.

- Sub-level categorisations are determined by

an expert in the field.

- Each expert manages a category or defines sub-categories and assigns managers to those sub-categories.

- Each category has a collection of external links to relevant WWW sites and internal links to pages associated with the category.

- Archaeologists' sites hosted within this 'soapbox site' should be accessible both by following the categories and via a direct link or URL; i.e., a user should be able to reach the site both by browsing the categories or by typing a site's direct URL.

- The user sites would be generated via a WWW-site 'engine' that would ensure an appealing look for each site.

- A storage limit would have to be defined, as a safeguard against malicious attempts to overload the site-hosting machine(s).

- An archaeologist with a site too large to be accommodated can always contact the soapbox administrator, requesting more space. Since the imposed limits are safeguard measures, not economical restrictions, the assignment of the extra space should prove no problem at all, in the majority of cases.

5 A previous WWW engine system

In order to develop efficiently WWW sites for museums, Morgado *et al.* (1999) created a system for generating sites based on content rather than structure. The structure was based on the concept of using an adjustable layout, capable of accepting plug-in modules that would present specific information in some way. These modules could be vertical menus, scrolling text frames, photo albums, and so on. This system was called a 'WWW-site engine'.

6 The programming structure of the original engine

The original engine's layout was structured in this way: every site would have an entry page and 5 sub-sections. Every page would have a top area for navigation and a bottom area for displaying information. Examples can be seen at the WWW sites for the Museum of Abade de Baçal, the Museum of the Iron Ore and of the Moncorvo Region, and other sites (see Table 1).

Figure 4 presents the entry page for the Museum of Mogadouro, in Trás-os-Montes, Northern Portugal. These areas were defined by the use of frames, which allow different files to be assigned to different screen areas. By coding these as Active Server Pages (ASP) the dynamic behaviour of the site could be assured. For example, the top navigation page must have a graphical element for the name of the current area. Using HTML or DHTML, this would be expressed as:

```
<IMG src="CurrentArea.GIF" txt="Current
Area">
```

However, using ASP, we create a database that holds the filenames, alternative text, links, etc. We can then query the database table (see Table 2) to obtain the information specific to each site.

ASP includes code within HTML by enclosing it within <% %> tags. A snippet of ASP code might be composed as follows. First, we open a connection to the database:

```
<%
Set ODBCasp = Server.CreateObject("ADODB
.Connection")
Session("id")=Request.QueryString("id")
ODBCasp.Open
```

```
"DSN=Museums;UID=WWWUser;PWD=WWWUserPass;
database=Museums"
SQLQueryasp="SELECT * FROM section Where
ID=" & session("id") & ""Set RSaspList =
ODBCasp.Execute(SQLQueryasp)
%>
```

These lines would place in the collection RSaspList, the data for the Museum whose id number was passed in the URL.

After this, we can use:

```
<IMG src="<%=RSaspList("Activities_Name")
%>"
txt="<%=RSaspList("Activities_Name_Txt")
%>">
```

This code is processed by the server and sent to the browser as static HTML. For instance, for the site with id 5, the client browser gets (see Figure 5):

```
<IMG src="Exhibitions.GIF"
txt="Exhibitions">
```

But for the site with id 12, the client browser would get, from the same file (Figure 6):

```
<IMG src="Activities.GIF"
txt="Actividades">
```

The engine then uses a folder tree to archive the required files (Figure 7).

The archive root is common to all sites, with sub-folders existing for each sub-section. Within a sub-section, each folder holds the files for a specific site. This folder tree, together with the database design, is one of the main sources of the non-variable number of sections of the engine.

For the museums' WWW sites, for instance, there were 5 sections: atrium or main page, collections, activities, contacts, free theme 1 and free theme 2. While this structure allowed a fair amount of customisation, it nevertheless required strict adherence to the predefined structure. This problem will be addressed below.

The root contained a file called index.asp, which is key to the operation of the engine. It must be called with a parameter, identifying the desired site. That parameter is then passed on to every file, as required, making the ASP code work as intended. This parameter makes the URL look a bit awkward, something like:

```
http://www.domain.com/sites/index.html?id=12
```

Figure 4: Area division on the original WWW engine's pages.

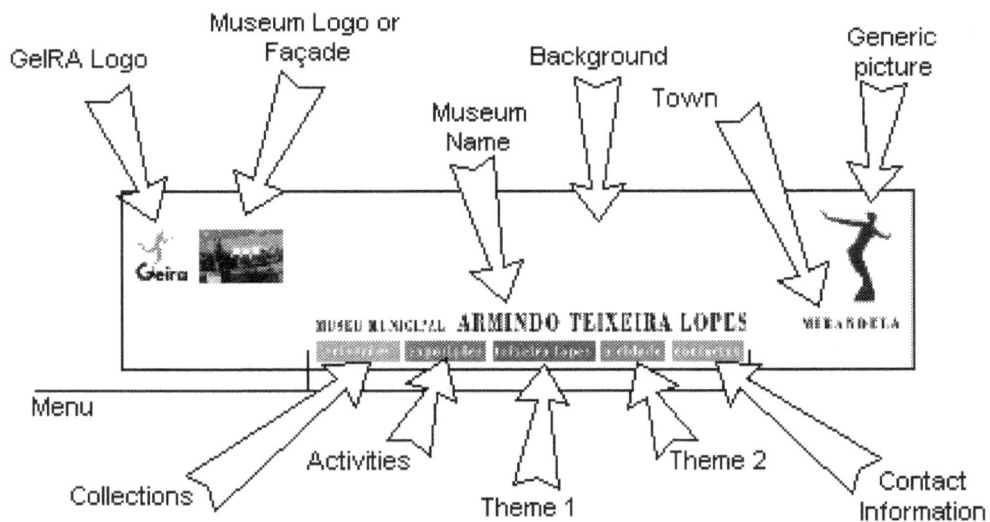

Figure 5: Navigational frame for museum id=5.

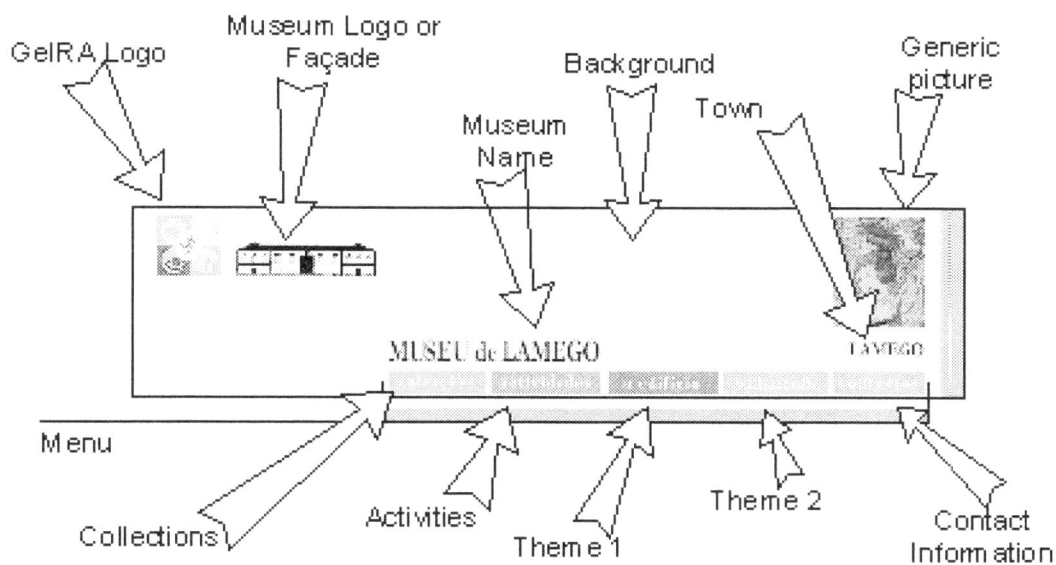

Figure 6: Navigational frame for museum id=12.

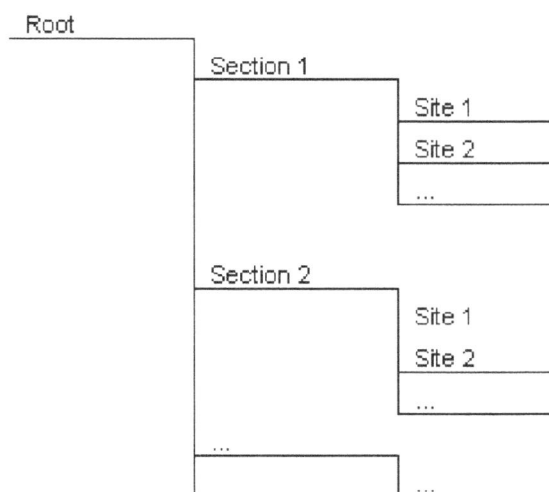

Figure 7: Folder structure of the original engine.

Site ID	Element Name	Value
5	Activities_Name	Exhibitions.GIF
5	Activities_Name_Txt	"Exhibitions"
12	Activities_Name	Activities.GIF
12	Activities_Name_Txt	"Activities"
...	...	...

Table 2: Table with the sites' elements.

A more common URL, such as

`http://www.domain.com/MySite`

is desired. This is achieved by having a single file in the /MySite root, that redirects the browser to the complex link. For older browsers (Netscape version 1, Internet Explorer versions 1 & 2), without JavaScript capabilities, a 'click here' message is displayed, requesting user intervention in order to jump to the appropriate URL.

7 Features that required modification

In order to improve the old engine, several features were desirable:

- a variable number of sub-sections or design elements per site.

- several layout designs to choose from.

- a larger number of plug-in modules.

- an interactive, simple interface.

- remote WWW administration.

8 The new WWW engine system

In order to make our engine more suitable for its intended purpose and to provide greater flexibility, we particularly wanted to have:

- a variable number of sub-sections and associated navigational buttons.

- several structural layouts to choose from.

- a variable number of design elements.

To achieve these goals, we felt it was necessary to address two main issues:

- folder structure, and

- database structure.

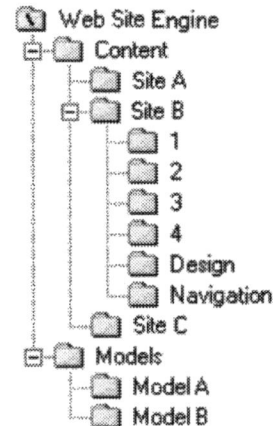

Figure 8: Folder structure of the current engine.

8.1 Folder structure

In the new structure, presented in Figure 8, there are only two folders within the root folder: one for content and the other for navigation models.

In the content folder, there is a sub-folder for each site. These sub-folders contain several other folders: one for navigation elements, another for design elements and one folder for each option present in the navigation frame. These 'option' folders are assigned numbers, indicating the option presentation sequence. For example, the first option to be displayed will have its files in the '1' folder, the second in the '2' folder, and so on. This allows for the automated addition of any number of folders, and also automated reordering on-the-fly.

8.2 Database entities

The WWW sites' content and models are stored in a single folder hierarchy; using the same approach, the sites' data and identification are stored in the same database as the models' data and identification. We chose the following as our database entities.

- WWW Sites
- Information Elements
- Navigation Elements
- Models
- Parameters

8.2.1 Database model

By establishing relationships between these entities, the database model is defined (Figure 9). To clarify how these entities work, our preliminary table definitions are given in Tables 3 to 7.

9 Engine operation

The addition of new sites is performed by the use of a specific Windows utility. A prototype of this engine is being used by UTAD for several archaeology sites presented via the IRAC '98 WWW site (see Table 1 for the URL).

First, one chooses the model to be used. Each one requires a different number of information/design elements, and will have different methods of deploying the navigation elements on the screen. After choosing the model, the utility checks the database to see what information/design elements are required. Values are then requested for these parameters. The same procedure is used for the navigation elements. These can vary in number, since the model only determines their organisation and operation.

By way of illustration, the model might have a top or side frame with navigation buttons and display the relevant pages in another frame. Or the model might have a start page with just some navigational elements that display the content in a frame set.

To include a navigation element, the only requirements are its position in the navigation element sequence, the files that belong to the associated sub-site and which one of those files is the index file. The utility can then copy the files into the folder structure of the engine. Should a resorting of the navigation elements be required, this is a simple task for the utility.

10 Creating WWW sites via the WWW

Since the utility is simply a form-based program, a WWW-based version can be programmed without major hurdles. The user task (that of the archaeologist) would be the supply of HTML and image files for each section. Since these are simply plugged into a navigation structure, the site is constructed with very little work other than text composition and image scanning. The Web sites constructed in this way are quite appealing both graphically and from a usability perspective. Examples of this can be seen at the archaeology sites developed at the UTAD, such as the IRAC '98 site (see Table 1).

11 Management of the index site

A search engine could automatically index the sites developed using our engine—indeed this could be a service of the engine itself. Keywords for the site (metadata) could be part of a model's parameters (see section 3 above).

However, the development of an index site is key to the entire project: its main structure must be defined by an archaeologist, each sub-section being managed and co-ordinated by an expert in the specific field. This would be a perfect project for inter-university co-operation, due to the high number of experts required and the potential for wide spread broadcast and classification of archaeological information.

12 Utilising our model

Having a working model and utility, the information required can be broken down into elements—framed text, image tables, and so on. Currently, these elements are available only as pieces of HTML code, usable by anyone, but requiring HTML expertise. By applying the engine model to WWW page construction, our overall aim is to achieve a much better graphic design and to ease the WWW site construction process.

References

[1] McGovern, G. 1999. Information Nobodies. *New Thinking E-Mail Newsletter*, 331. http://www.nua.ie/newthinking/archives/-newthinking331/index.html, Accessed 27/01/00.

[2] Miller, P. 1996. An application of Dublin Core from the Archaeology Data Service. http://ads.ahds.ac.uk/project/metadata/d-ublin.html), Accessed 27/01/00. Un-

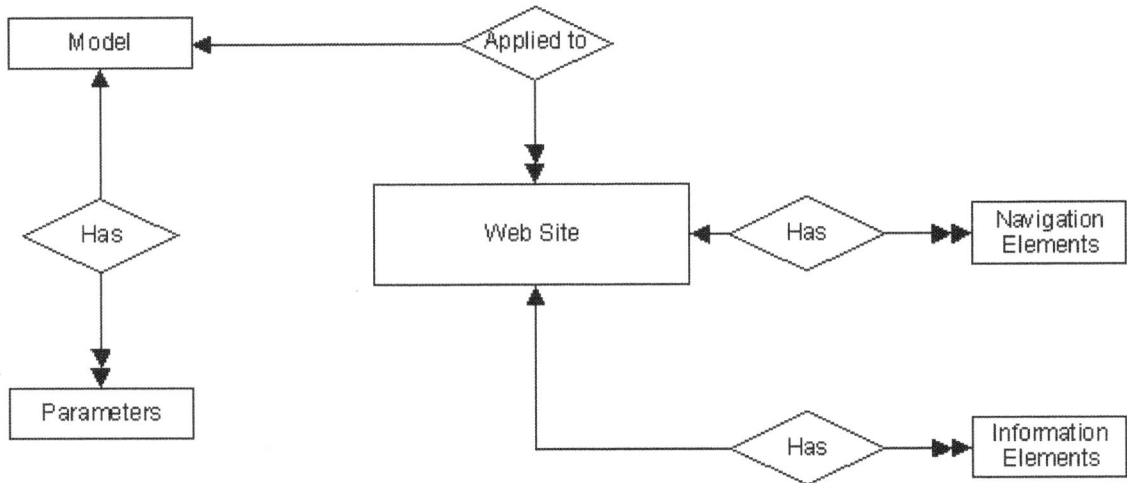

Figure 9: Database model of the engine.

SITES			
ID	**Title**	**TemplateID**	**Location**
Identifier	Site title: text to be displayed in the title area of the browser window.	Id of the design model to be used when rendering this site.	Folder containing the site, in the \Content folder.

Table 3: Preliminary definition of the 'WWW Site' entity in Figure 9.

INFORMATION ELEMENTS				
ID	**SiteID**	**AltTag**	**ImageSrc**	**Anchor**
Identifier.	Id of the site this element belongs to.	Text to be displayed as an element if no image is available, or as an alt tag, otherwise.	Image to be displayed. If left empty, element content will be the content of the AltTag field.	A tag (hypertext anchor) to be associated with the element (if desired). Allows definition of a bookmark or hyperlink (both with and without target frame).

Table 4: Prelimininary definition of the 'Information Elements' entity in Figure 9.

NAVIGATION ELEMENTS				
ID	**SiteID**	**AltTag**	**ImageSrc**	**Sequence**
Identifier.	Id of the site this element belongs to.	Text to be displayed as an element if no image is available, or as an alt tag, otherwise.	Image to be displayed. If left empty, element content will be the content of the AltTag field.	Position of the navigation element on all lists. Also the name of the folder with the files of the area it represents. Selecting an information element displays the index.html file in that folder. Target frame or bookmark is determined by the site's design model.

Table 5: Preliminary definition of the 'Navigation Elements' entity in Figure 9.

48

MODELS			
ID	**Name**	**Num_Param**	**Location**
Identifier.	Model Identification	Number of set-up parameters required for operation of this model. The function of each parameter is defined in the model's files.	Folder containing the model's files (within the \Models folder).

Table 6: Preliminary definition of the 'Model' entity in Figure 9.

PARAMETERS				
ID	**ModelID**	**SiteID**	**Name**	**Value**
Identifier.	Model using this parameter.	Site for which the entry's value is valid.	Parameter id.	Parameter value, of use to the model ModelID, on the site SiteID.

Table 7: Preliminary definition of the 'Parameters' entity in Figure 9.

published document from University of Newcastle, UK.

[3] Morgado, L., Reis, A., Abreu, M., Bicho, J., Santos, A., Guedes, M., Barroso, J., Melo-Pinto, P., Lobo, H. amd Proença, A. and Bulas-Cruz, J. 1999. A web site engine for the development of heritage-related sites. In J. Barceló, I. Briz and A. Vila, (eds.), *New Techniques for Old Times. CAA98: Computer Applications and Quantitative Methods in Archaeology. Proceedings of the 26th conference, Barcelona 1998*, pp. 369–70, Oxford. British Archaeological Reports International Series 757.

[4] van Leusen, M., Champion, S., Lizee, J. and Plunkett, T. 1996. Toward a European Archaeological Heritage Web. In H. Kamermans and K. Fennema, (eds.), *Interfacing the Past: Computer applications and quantitative methods in archaeology CAA 95*, Leiden. Analecta Praehistorica Leidensia 28. http://odur.let.rug.nl/ arge/Docs/eahw.html, Accessed 27/01/00.

[5] Weibel, S., Godby, J., Miller, E. and Daniel, R. 1995. *OCLC/NCSA Metadata Workshop Report.* Dublin (US), Online Computer Library Center. http://www.oclc.org:5046/oclc/research/conferences/metadata/dublin_core_report.html, Accessed 27/01/00.

A numismatic database with icon and string-searching features

Leonel Morgado and Mário Guedes

GeIRA Project

University of Trás-os-Montes e Alto Douro - Computer Centre

Quinta de Prados, 5000 Vila Real, Portugal

email: leonelm@utad.pt

1 Introduction

The Museum of Vila Real has a prized collection of over 50,000 ancient coins, the result of many years of devoted effort by Father João Parente, who donated his collection to the town. Parente (1997) published part of the collection in a tome containing numismatic data for 5,000 coins and photographs of 1100 of these (Figure 1).

The museum staff felt it would be desirable to make the Parente numismatic database available via the World-Wide-Web (WWW). To do this, it was necessary to create an electronic database from the information illustrated in Figure 1. Of all the information to be encoded, it is that labelled 'MARK' which caused the greatest problems. The 'marks' on the coins consist of schema with distinctive letters or scripts that could not immediately be encoded as text.

2 Storing the marks in the database

Most marks consist of letters set in a frame. For instance, in Figure 1, the string 'SMNA' under a horizontal line forms a mark; however, a large number of coins have symbols among the letters (Figure 2).

One of the first approaches was to store the marks as images but there were several drawbacks.

- Scanning would be a tedious process, lacking enough similarities to automate the process.

- The book binding would have to be destroyed to get a regular orientation of the marks.

- The extension of each coins' text information (description of faces, notes, and so on) varies greatly, making it difficult to vertically locate a mark on any given page.

- Storing the marks as images doesn't allow for text or symbol searches.

Analysis of the structure of the mark schemas showed that the symbols could in large part be represented by alphanumeric characters. A random sampling of several dozen marks revealed four different schemas, indicating that the total number of schemas was low enough to allow specific processing of each type. Figure 3 displays the four types of schema found, the letter 'A' representing various strings.

The book contained few non-Roman coins. These non-Roman coins had no schemas registered in the book (for these, the book contained a single horizontal line, '-', in the 'MARK' column). Therefore, we have not tried to deal with the problem of registering non-Roman schemas. However, as long as the number of schemas is low enough to allow specific processing for each one, this system can be expanded to accommodate them. This would be quite easy to achieve: imagine a fifth kind of schema, with N strings, each occupying a particular position. A specific processing would be developed for it, which would take care of the organisation and display issues. The string association would be accomplished by simply inserting the N strings in the Fields_Marca table (also see Figure 5).

Each schema has its own organisation and a specific number of alphanumeric strings that are reflected in the database structure. Three database tables are used to store such data as follows.

- **Moedas** (Coins), containing the basic prop-

N.	Type	OBVERSE	REVERSE	MARK WEIGHT	AXIS DIAMETERS	ORIGIN	REFERENCES NOTES
3ᴿᴰ GROUP 1ˢᵗ *officina*							
2220	*Aes* 4	D N CONSTAN-TINVS P F AVG Diademed head with laurels and rosettes, to the right	GLOR-IA EXERC-ITVS Two soldiers and a standard	⎯⎯⎯ SMNA 1.074	12 h 15/15.6	Vila Marim	RIC 7; LRBC 1134

Figure 1: Numismatic data from Father Parente's book, published in 1997 (translated).

Figure 2: Some symbols found in the coins' marks.

erties of the coins.

- **Formato_marca** (Mark Format), containing the schemas of the marks' strings.

- **Fields_marca** (Mark Fields), containing the strings used in a marks' schema.

These three tables are then linked via the following relationships. Each coin (an item in the Moedas table) is associated with a schema (an item in the Formato_marca table) and with a variable number of strings (items in the Fields_Marca table). This allows the creation of a data entry and query form for marks. As the mark types are limited, the form automatically adapts for each by drawing the divider elements and creating or eliminating fields for string insertion and display. The actual structure of the tables is described later.

At this stage in the database construction process, the main issue was to find ways to store and retrieve the symbols recorded in the 'MARK' column. By visiting the company that performed the page composition (typesetting) of the book by Father Parente (1997), we obtained the computer files used. These were page layout files, that could not be used to retrieve the coin information itself. This was because the information that made up each page was simply laid out graphically; like paper cutouts on a sheet. No connection was available between pieces of text, images, etc. However, the symbols present in the book were stored by this company in GIF files; one for each image (for information about this and other image formats see Miano 1999). Exploration of these GIF files yielded a full set of binary

image symbols. There are 96 altogether (including laurel wreaths, diamonds, mirrored letters, aggregated letters, and so on). These 96 symbols, the 26 letters of the alphabet and the 10 numeric characters give 132 different items that can be displayed by using single-byte fonts.

A further option was the creation of a new font set which included characters found in the coin-marks (dropping ã, Ç, £, §, and others). This uses considerably less disk space than storing images, and allows for fast searching of mark components. The data entry process is also much faster than any current optical scanning process.

The font we designed is a TrueType vector font, created using Corel Draw (Dickman 1999). This software offers on-line help with full information on how to use it for TrueType font creation. Our font is available for use by interested third parties (please email us at the address at the head of this paper).

Database operators can easily enter the mark definition information because the coin-mark insertion form includes an active table with all available symbols. An operator just has to use the keyboard for normal characters and make mouse clicks on appropriate icons for symbols (Figure 4). A similar form can be used to define searches of the database for instances of a particular symbol (see below).

Regarding future expansion of this method, should a particular situation demand more than the 256 characters available on single-byte fonts, it is technically possible to convert the system to Unicode two-byte fonts (Unicode Consortium 2000). This kind of font encoding allows for 65636 characters per font, and is commonly used

A A A A	A A A A A A	A │ A A │ A A A	A │ A A │ A A A
1 upper string; 1 lower string	2 upper strings; 1 lower string	2 upper strings split by divider, 1 lower string	4 upper strings split by divider, 1 lower string

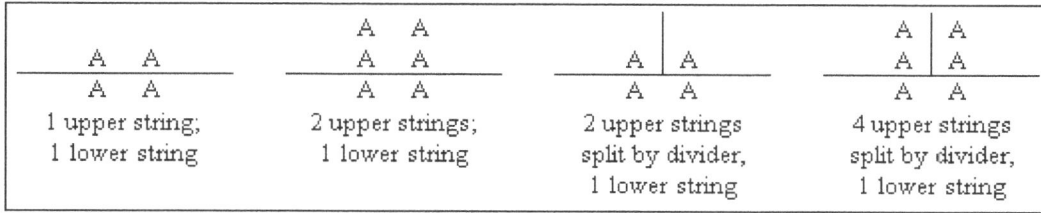

Figure 3: Four schemas found in a random sample.

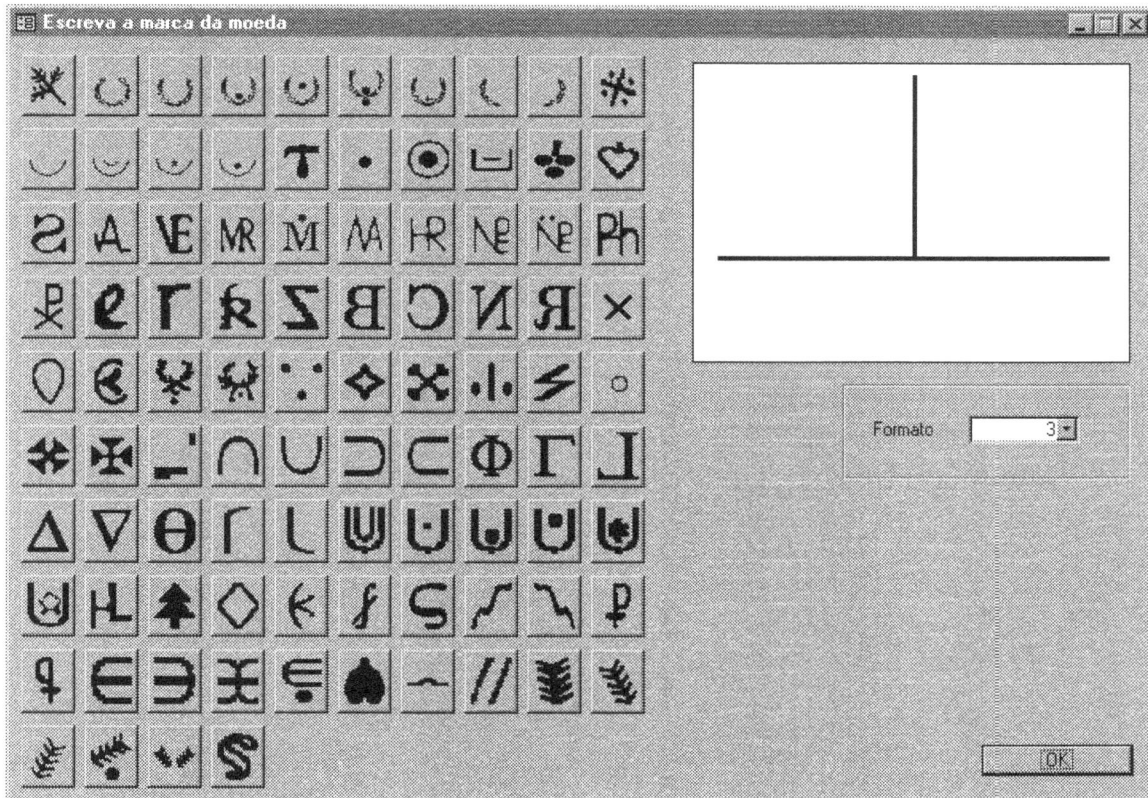

Figure 4: Coin-mark insertion form.

in the computer science field for encoding oriental languages. Of course, the interface would also have to be redesigned to allow useful organisation of such a vast collection of symbols. But these issues go beyond the aim of the current paper.

3 Database structure

The database was designed not as a definitive concept, but rather as support for the computer archiving of the Parente numismatic information. We have achieved this in such a way as to allow further refinement and processing, or exporting of information into other specialised database software. For this purpose, the database was designed using the Boyce-Codd normalised form. Normalisation is a process of eliminating duplication and inconsistencies from a database, right from the database design phase. This renders the database structure readily convertible into a different format, and improves the longevity and usability of its data. Information about Boyce-Codd normalisation is readily available in most college manuals on database design. Gupta (1996) authored a site with normalisation information, including the Boyce-Codd normal form. The resulting database organisation is presented in Figure 5.

As an example, no special codes or text are used to indicate that a particular coin is a *denarius* or some other kind of Roman coin. A table ('Tipos') holds a list of types, including the *denarius*, and assigns each a unique numerical identifier, that is used as the key value in the relationship between the coins table ('Moedas') and the types table. Therefore, assume you need to convert a coin to another database: looking at the 'Moeda' table, you get a type value of '1'. Checking the table 'Tipos', you get the textual information (Table 1). This immediately tells you that all coins labelled with type '1' are *denarii*. Therefore, a conversion table, of the look-up kind, is easily constructed. Common Structured Query Language (SQL) queries (ISO 1992) can then be used to convert the database to any other normalised format. Even in the case of a format that falls short of Boyce-Codd normalisation, conversion is possible, by developing a program to perform the conversion. What matters is that the information structure allows these conversions to be performed automatically, with no need for human intervention at the record level.

In addition, should the need arise to associate our mark-storage method with another database format, such as that of Volk (1995), this can eas-

ID	Description
1	*Denarius*
...	...

Table 1: Snapshot of the 'Tipos' table.

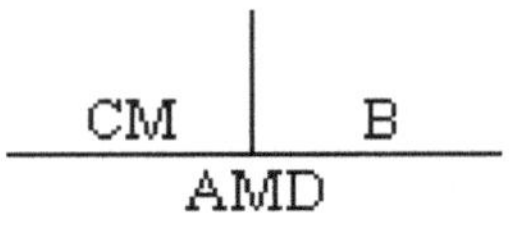

CM	B

AMD

Figure 6: Fictitious mark used in the example.

ily be done. All that is required is to create a matching table between the original database and the mark-storage method tables. Since Terence Volk's database structure is not normalised, programming is required to convert data in our format to his. Such code would be centred in the generation of the identification strings used by Volk. Lookup tables and conversion procedures can then be constructed to convert the numeric codes used here to the substrings used in Volk's identification strings, such as 'ROMN' for Roman coins, 'rpb' for republic, and so forth. An interesting project would be to convert Volk's database to a normalised format. Such work is, however, beyond the scope of this paper.

Our tables that address the mark-schema storage issue are unusual and require further explanation. Tables 2 and 3 present their internal structure. To clarify the usage of these tables, let us consider an example, the representation of a fictitious mark (Figure 6). This example mark has 3 strings. These will have three entries in the Fields_marca table (Table 4). The FormType column indicates that string '1' has the value 'CM', is in the first position of the schema number 3 and belongs to coin number 5436. The same kind of reading can be applied to strings '2' and '3'. The full schema is shown in Table 5.

There is a technical issue here, regarding the storage of images in databases. Our database was originally developed in Microsoft Access 97 (Viescas 1996), so we used its internal 'OLE Object' field (Chappel 1996). However, for our WWW pages we use a more powerful database system, Microsoft SQL Server (Delaney and Soukup 1999), which does not possess that data type. However, since what we need in order to display an image is the binary data that composes

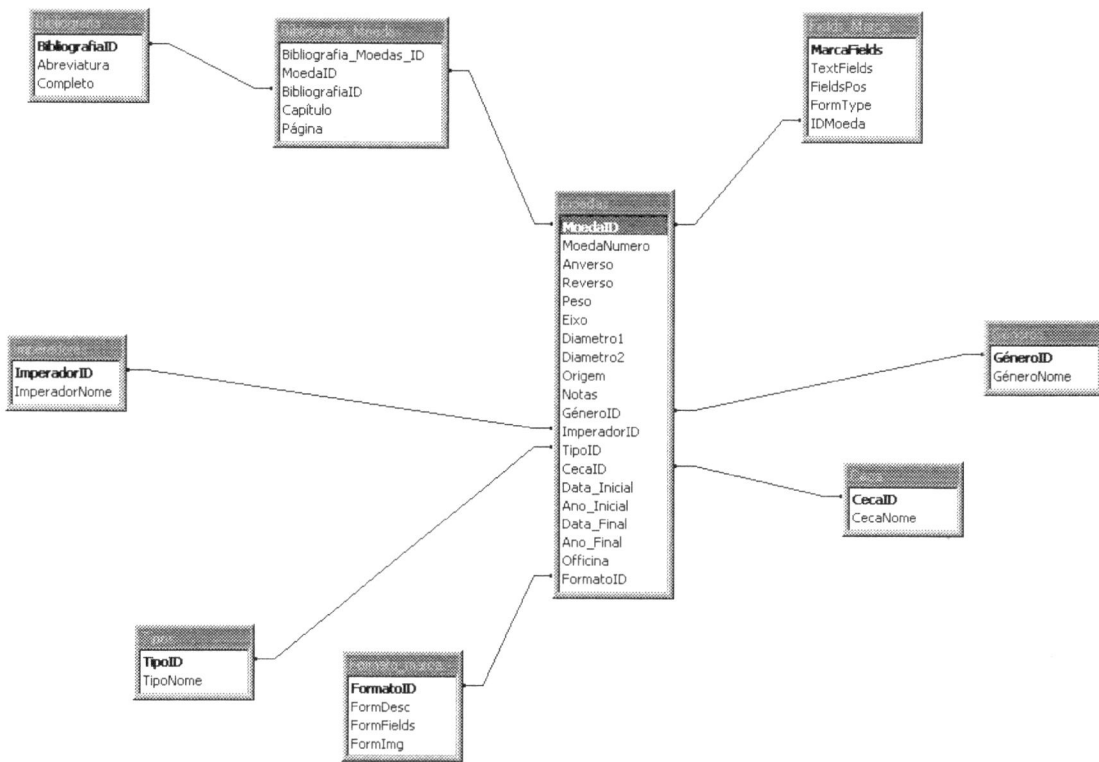

Figure 5: The database structure.

Fields_marca		
FIELD NAME	**TYPE**	**DESCRIPTION**
MarcaFields	Numeric	Unique ID field.
TextFields	Text	Text string to be displayed.
FieldsPos	Numeric	Ordinal position of the field within a schema.
FormType	Numeric	Schema in which this field is used.
IDMoeda	Numeric	ID of the coin this field

Table 2: Internal structure of the 'Fields_marca' table.

Formato_marca		
FIELD NAME	**TYPE**	**DESCRIPTION**
FormatoID	Numeric	Unique ID field.
FormDesc	Text	Text description of the schema.
FormFields	Numeric	Number of fields within the schema.
FormImg	OLE Object / Binary Data	Image associated with the schema (for background in visual forms, also useful as an extra description, etc.).

Table 3: Internal structure of the 'Formato_marca' table.

MarcaFields	TextFields	FieldsPos	FormType	IDMoeda
1	CM	1	3	5436
2	B	2	3	5436
3	AMD	3	3	5436
...	...	...	...	...

Table 4: The 'Fields_marca' entries for the example.

FormatoID	FormDesc	FormFields	FormImg
...	...	...	...
3	2 upper strings split by divider; 1 lower string	3	
...	...	...	...

Table 5: The 'Formato_marca' entry for the example.

56

it, we can store this in the SQL Server database in the form of a GIF image file (for information about this and other image formats see Miano 1999). This image format is one of the most widely used in the world, and is supported by all graphical WWW browsers and most image-editing software.

Another simple option would be the storage of filenames. We did not follow this option, however, since keeping the entire information in the database provides more reliability regarding its longevity: files detached from the main database can easily be corrupted, lost, etc.

4 Database querying and longevity

Since the database is normalised, it can be queried using standard SQL commands (ISO 1992). This allows both simple and complex queries to be created. The most practical way of using them is to create graphical interfaces, such as forms in Microsoft Access 97 or WWW-based forms, to execute each specific kind of query. For instance, if one wants to retrieve all coins struck by the second *officina* of the mint of Milan, an interface can be developed to behave as follows.

Let us assume that Milan has ID 4 in the mint table ('Ceca'). In this case, the coins from Milan have the number '4' in the CecaID field. Thus, the following query would retrieve the ID numbers of the desired coins (bold lettering indicates SQL commands).

SELECT MoedaID **FROM** moedas **WHERE** CecaID=4 **AND** Officina=2;

Of course, this would be best performed via a form. The form would contain a list box or a clickable map, to allow the user to choose the mint; and an edit box, to allow them to enter the *officina* number. The form code would then generate the SQL command string above, and query the various database tables to present the desired information (i.e. the emperor's name, not its code, and the visual mark, not its coding).

Now, suppose that you want to find all the instances of coins with a particular symbol. By using a form such as the one in Figure 4, it is easy to select the desired symbol. Since a character in the font represents that symbol, say '§', a SQL query can easily retrieve the desired information:

SELECT DISTINCT IDMoeda **FROM** Fields_marca **WHERE** TextFields **LIKE** '%§%';

This query would retrieve all ID numbers of the coins in whose marks the symbol represented by '§' turns up. Notice that the retrieved field is ID-Moeda, from the Fields_marca table (which is the table being queried). Constructing queries such as these is extremely simple in graphical database interfaces such as that of Microsoft's Access 97 and others with visual interfaces.

Regarding data longevity, all the fields are readily imported into most modern databases, since they use only common data formats—the alphanumeric text fields are short, all numbers are integers, and so on. The only potential question regarding longevity is posed by the storage of schema images in the Formato_marca table. No standard data format exists for images, each software vendor provides a different solution. However, most databases allow raw binary data to be stored. As explained above, this allows storage of images as GIF or JPEG files. Thus, in the most extreme case, the image data could be extracted from the database and placed in separate files, for use in some other fashion.

Another issue is the risk of losing the actual font, which, in fact, is the only element connecting a symbol to the character that is stored in the strings of the Fields_marca table. We have not addressed this problem, but some possible approaches have occurred to us. One of the following may, in the future, yield a solution.

- Creation of a table associating text characters with descriptions of the symbols they represent and raw binary data images of each.

- Storage of one or several fonts in a database table. This would allow different single-byte fonts to be used for different sets of coins or marks. An extra column could be added to the Fields_marca table, associating a field with the font that should be used to display it.

5 Presentation on the WWW

Our special font would not be suited for delivery via the WWW because different Internet clients have diverse font-support capabilities. In addition, new trends in television set top boxes may result in millions of new WWW users who have limited or no font-downloading capabilities at all. As the symbols are monochrome and quite small, GIF images of each would download rapidly. Thus, this was the solution we adopted.

The server-side scripting used for the database

queries detects when a particular character requires an image and includes it where necessary in the HTML code. The Museum's WWW site uses Active Server Page scripts but this technique can be employed with any WWW-scripting technology (CGI, Perl, and so on). Work on the on-line database is still on going and is very much experimental at present, but we welcome you to observe our progress with the site at http://www.utad.geira.pt/museus/vilareal/.

6 Acknowledgements

This project is sponsored by the EU programmes Interreg II (02/REGII/6/96), Feder and, the FCT (Foundation for Science and Technology).

References

[1] Chappel, D. 1996. *Understanding ActiveX and OLE*. USA, Microsoft Press.

[2] Delaney, K. and Soukup, R. 1999. *Inside Microsoft SQL Server 7.0*. USA, Microsoft Press.

[3] Dickman, C. 1999. *Mastering Corel Draw 9*. California, USA, Alameda.

[4] Gupta, G. 1996. Normalisation. (http://www.cs.jcu.edu.au/ftp/web/teaching/Subjects/cp1500/1997/Lecture_Notes/normalisation/contents.html), Accessed 8/1/00.

[5] Miano, J. 1999. *Compressed Image File Formats: JPEG, PNG, GIF, XBM, BMP*. New York, USA, ACM Press.

[6] Parente, J. 1997. *Museu de Vila Real - Moedas - Tomo I*. Vila Real, Câmara Municipal de Vila Real.

[7] Unicode Consortium, (ed.) 2000. *The Unicode Standard, Version 3*. Montain View, California, USA, The Unicode Consortium.

[8] Viescas, J. 1996. *Running Access 97*. USA, Microsoft Press.

[9] Volk, T. 1995. Retroconversion and the numerical analysis of Roman republican coin-hoards, part I. *Rivista Italiana di Numismatica XCVI*, pp. 105–186.

Electronic drawing or manual drawing? Experiences from work with rock-paintings

Emma Jane Read[†] **and Christopher Chippindale**[*]

[†]Cambridge University Department of Archaeology

Downing Street, Cambridge, CB2 3DZ, United Kingdom

[†]email: er1007@cam.ac.uk

[*]Cambridge University Museum of Archaeology and Anthropology

Downing Street, Cambridge, CB2 3DZ, United Kingdom

[*]North Australian Research Unit/Department of Archaeology and Anthropology

Australian National University, Canberra ACT 0200, Australia

[*]email: cc43@cam.ac.uk

1 Introduction: rock-art recording and the electronic opportunity

A revolution in the capacities and availability of computers and software over the past decade has made powerful technology available to most researchers. Just as word-processing has become cheap and accessible, so now are technologies relating to graphics and image-processing. The hardware (PCs, scanners, printers), the size of files (tens of megabytes for a single colour image), the quantity of RAM to work effectively with them (again typically tens of megabytes), and powerful software (starting with Adobe Photoshop) are now within the scope of the moderately resourced researcher using routine kit in a university department. In parallel with these developments, electronic media—CD-ROM publications, Web sites, news-groups, publications and journals—have also started to play a significant role in the work of most researchers.

Even in the not many months between this paper being presented at the Cardiff conference in spring 1999 and its publication in April 2000, the electronic world has yet again moved on. The hardware and software used for this study, then reasonably up to date, are now decidedly obsolete. The new machines are once again faster, with more RAM and larger hard discs. Once again the largest size of file that is convenient to work with, to store or to transfer between machines has decidedly increased. It is still necessary to strike a balance between file-size and image resolution, but the point of balance now involves less compromise of image quality. One is coming a little closer to the point at which one can specify an image quality exactly suiting what graphic work will be done, and then work with whatever file-size is thereby required. The parallel with text processing applies: within a decade of its coming into universal use, word-processing software on standard hardware has now reached such power that the average academic user need pay no attention at all to file size, to how long a file takes to save, or to how complex is its formatting. You just do what you want, and the machine copes.

Digital cameras are again cheaper and more powerful; the remark made below—that for most rock-art field studies digital cameras do not match conventional 35 mm photography followed by digitization—remains true, but it will not for much longer. It chances that the present authors both work largely in remote regions, of India and Australia, where they are not in easy and daily contact with mains electricity. The continuing advantage for us of conventional photography is that stored images take the form of exposed canisters of 35 mm film. Digital cameras, with their limited storage, need either to be plugged in to a computer on-site, or downloaded on to one frequently. In a field season we have used as many as 150 films of 37 exposures each, or some 5500 frames. That many films are conveniently carried in a stuff-bag. Assuming a file-size of 100 Megabytes per image, that number of images amounts to 550 Gigabytes. That was once a staggering quantity of data. The iMac on which the present text is being revised has the standard disc-size of about 6 Gigabytes, so there is a ratio of about 100 fold between the standard disc-capacity and the typical need for a field season's records. As disc-space becomes rapidly cheaper, one can see that discrepancy bridged before long.

An area of archaeology where graphics is central is in rock-art. Conventionally, the field record of rock-art is made with photographs and tracings in some combination, from which a considered image is arrived at by manual drawing (Sanger and Meighan 1990). Some other disciplines where accurate drawing is essential, such as architecture, are nearly fully electronic in their routine drawing; the same habit will surely arrive in rock-art studies.

Electronic graphics have their own vocabulary, much of it broadly equivalent to that used for manual graphics. Some is novel. We were not entirely surprised when an expert referee for this volume did not understand the difference between a bitmap and a grayscale image as we have used it. Both are monochrome, that is degrees of dark and light within the same colour. Generally, the colour is black, so the monochrome range is from pure black (full presence) to pure white (full absence); it can be any colour, so red to white, blue to white, or whatever. The difference is that a bitmap image permits only presence and absence, the black (or solid colour) and the white: it is the electronic equivalent of a line drawing. A grayscale image permits a great many intermediate tones of grey (for a black-and-white image): it is the electronic equivalent of a conventional black-and-white photograph. (The referee pointed out that a bitmap image is one that contains values for each individual pixel, as opposed to, say, a vector image. However, in Photoshop, as a graphics program which works with pixel images rather than vector images, bitmap is used with the meaning reported in this paragraph.)

2 Drawing rock-engravings and drawing rock-paintings

Rock-engravings were made by cutting away the surface of the rock, by hammering, pecking, gouging or scratching, to leave an archaeological trace as an area of modified rock surface. Although portions of figures may vary very much in depth, they are generally recorded as a figure of cut rock-surface distinguished from a ground of uncut rock-surface. This is generally treated as an absolute difference between image and ground: so the figure cut into the rock is drawn absolute black, and the ground of the unmarked rock surface is the paper left absolute white. The engravings as images in absolute black and white are binary in electronic terms. In graphic work this means treating images as bitmap rather than as grayscale images. This is a fair approximation but not a perfect one, for the area of solid black does not show the difference in depth or in texture that exists in a rock-engraving. On some surfaces, recorders can discern when one figure cuts another and must be later. Using a simple binary technique, it is hard to show clearly what is going on when different engravings of different depths run together or cut across each other; that can, with difficulty, be done by using greys or a different style of indicating individual peckmarks (see Figure 1).

Deep rock-engravings are observed today by their depth and profile. Shallow rock-engravings are observed by their colour or tone: they look darker or lighter or have a different texture by comparison with the unmarked rock. The difference sometimes arises from an actual difference in the colour or tone of the rock surface, sometimes a striking one, because the surface where marked has not re-established a surface appearance exactly like that in areas where the marking was not made. Sometimes it is emphasized further by micro-organisms that darken or change the colour of the engraved zone. Or shadows and differences in cross-light throw the engraved area, a fraction lower than the adjacent surface, into partial and sufficient shadow. These are all secondary effects from the fundamental, that an engraving is generally detected by its three-dimensional relief. The way forward for engraving, then, is the developing of accurate recording methods (RAPP 2000, 94 ff.) for three-dimensional surfaces. That record once made, the data-processing issue will be the development of algorithmic methods to judge just where the natural surface profile is broken by the cut of the engraving.

Rock-paintings are also typically drawn in black and white. Unlike engravings, paintings only sometimes approximate to a binary image, of a solid area of even-coloured paint against an even background of rock. For monochrome images, an area of solid black conventionally denotes the painted surface of the figure, however variable is the tone or the strength of pigment across the image. When a figure has been executed in polychrome it is recorded in black and white: different textures of black ink can be used to denote different colours, but it is hard to convey effectively the impression of polychrome (see Plates 1 and 2). Whilst this method of recording often helps to elucidate a motif, in the process information about colour tone, hue and texture are largely lost.

At some point, the conventional record becomes so far removed from the real as to become a technical drawing, no kind of substitute for the original art because so abstracted from it (see Leibhammer 1998; Nettleton 1985; Skotnes 1994; Molyneaux 1997; Bradley 1997a).

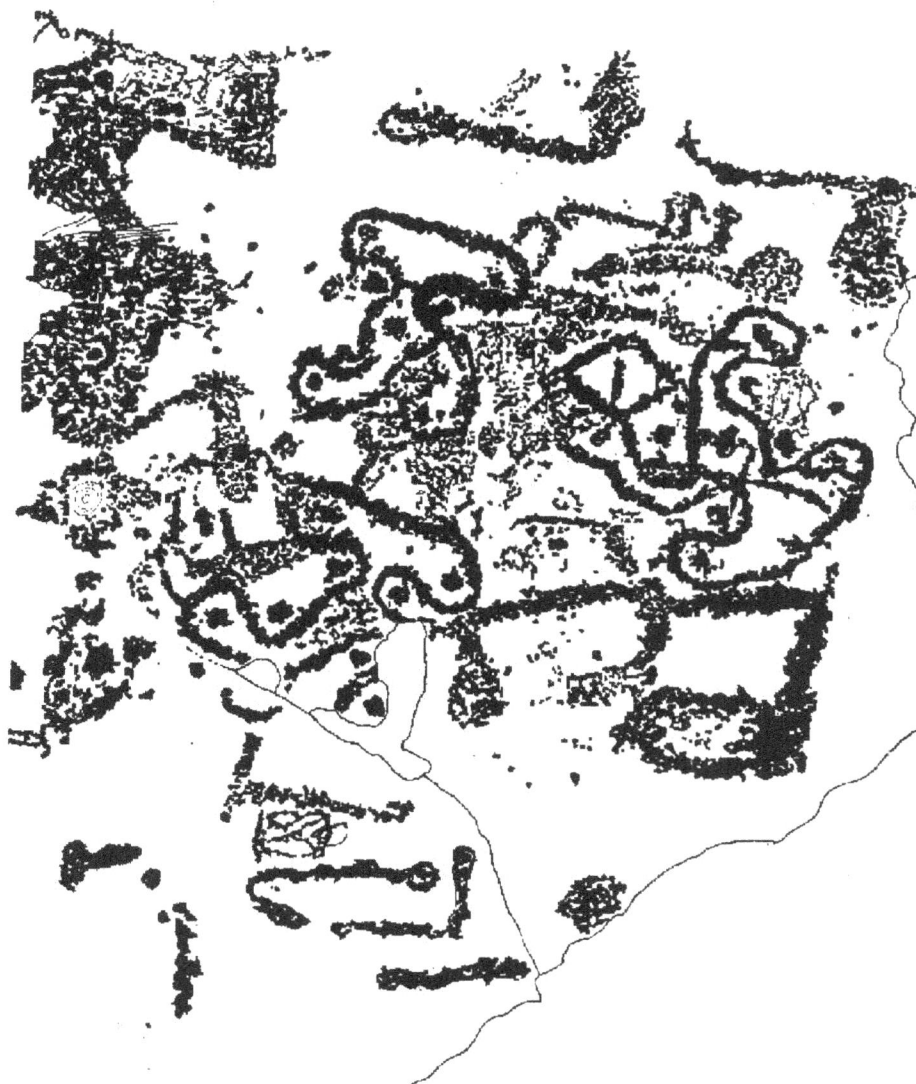

Figure 1: An example of a drawing taken from a rock-engraving, Luine, rock 30-B, Valcamonica, Italy. Information about different phases of rock-engraving is included by nuances in how the engraved area is drawn. Reproduced from Anati (1994, 84) by scanning the printed book.

The issue of how we visualize rock-art motifs, panels and sites is an area ripe for debate. Whilst many rock-art researchers are aware of these problems (see Brayer *et al.* 1998; Layton 1991; Clegg 1991; Tilley 1991; Bégouën and Clottes 1987) the requirements of traditional publishing methods have meant that black-and-white images remain the principal method of documenting and therefore of understanding rock-art.

3 The potential of computer-aided studies in rock-art

The contribution that computers can make to rock-art have been discussed since the early 1980s (for example Rip 1983; 1989; Dickman 1984) and more recently computer-aided documentation methods have been evolved by several researchers (Arcà and Bulas Cruz 1998; Brayer *et al.* 1998; Clogg and Díaz-Andreu 1998; Arcà 1998; Donnan 1998; Firnhaber 1998; Bertani *et al.* 1997; Henderson 1995; Bednarik and Seshadri 1995). An International Rock Art Database Project has been proposed (Walt *et al.* 1997)

This article has attempted to incorporate the power and flexibility of the now available graphics packages into the drawing of rock-art. The scope of these packages is great; they provide highly effective tools for enhancing and manipulating the presentation of images. The equivalents to these techniques have long been available to professional photographers through conventional photographic retouching and colour adjustment. The electronic techniques have the extra benefit that one sees, immediately and in colour, the results of any adjustments on-screen, and one can cancel or revise each manipulation if it does not do what is wanted. Whilst these techniques at first required one to develop one's own software, the standard programs are now enormously powerful and flexible. As has previously been the case for other software such as the varied databases developed for archaeological and museum applications, those specialized programs are being overtaken by the industry-standard generalized programs suitably used and sometimes suitably customized. The software is available at a reasonable cost, and it is user-friendly.

This study will look first at the ability of these packages to enhance images and then at their ability to actually aid in the drawing process. We used Adobe Photoshop, the standard graphics program for manipulating photographic and equivalent images. We used version 5.0 of Photoshop (dating to 1998); the current version (in March 2000) is a much-changed version 5.5 (see Table 1 for the URL). Photoshop is rapid and easy to use with a few of its controls (Adobe 1998); it permits a great deal of user adjustment, and there is much more to be learnt to use its full potential (see for example Adobe 1999; Evening 2000; Weinmann and Lourekas 1999).

4 Image enhancement

Photoshop enables one to enhance the quality of photographs after they have been developed, thereby assisting the researcher in documenting and interpreting images. Though not directly 'drawing' with Photoshop, these techniques are useful in preparing slides or colour prints for drawing or publication. At a first level, the 'Brightness' and 'Contrast' commands alongside the 'Sharpen' mask enable one to enhance photographs of rock-art sites that have not been developed to your satisfaction, perhaps appearing too dark (underexposed) or too light (overexposed), with too much or too little contrast, and/or unclear (Firnhaber 1998). From our experience we recommend use of these tools manually (as 'Levels' and 'Curves' and 'Unsharp') rather than making use of the 'Auto' function. These processes correct a photograph, much as conventional photographic processing can.

At a second level, in the study of rock-art images, and especially of faded images, the manipulation of 'Balance' and 'Contrast' within 'Color Channels', sometimes allows you to recover from confused present-day survivals a clear and considered image of what once was. A good precedent is a study at a north-western US rock-art site: there an incomprehensible spread of ochre across a painted surface was resolved into two distinct and reasonably clear motifs which had been overpainted and had run together (Merrell 1998; see also Arcà 1998; Donnan 1998; Clogg and Díaz-Andreu 1998). Through these processes our perception of the image is transformed, and we better know what the shape of the image is and was.

For example, the simple use of the 'Invert' command in Photoshop will turn a dark red rock-painting on a pale red background into a light blue image on a dark blue background (Plates 3 and 4). For many people, light on dark is easier to see than dark on light. Many men, like one of us, have a degree of colour blindness and find it easier to judge nuances of tone in blue than in red. Taken together, these lead us to find exploring the shape of an obscure dark red

Plate 1: Photograph of a famous scene from the Game Pass shelter, Drakensberg, South Africa: eland with an animal-headed human figure standing by its tail. As is characteristic of the more elaborate paintings in South Africa, it is executed in polychrome, and there are noticeable variations in the tone and strength of colour even within areas painted with the same pigment. Reproduced by scanning a 35 mm slide.

Plate 2: A drawing of the scene from the Game Pass shelter (Plate 1). It was originally printed in a red-brown on a buff-yellow, colours closer to the art and its surround in the field, than the black on white we reprint in here.
Reproduced from Lewis-Williams and Dowson (1989, 50) by scanning the printed book and converting the file to bitmap from colour. Some detail has been lost in reproducing from the printed book, as is increasingly the case as images are promiscuously and repeatedly printed out, scanned in, compressed, expanded, and transferred between programs.

Plate 3: A photograph of a faded ochre rock-painting, northern Australia, dark red patchy ochre on red sandstone. Reproduced by scanning a 35 mm slide.

Plate 4: Plate 3 after inversion (so red becomes blue and dark becomes light) and adjustments to the blue channel. Manipulated in Photoshop.

figure on lighter rock better when it is inverted into blue and light on dark. In this study, we inverted an Australian image; doing this allowed us to see clearly the profile of the head of the figure, previously understood erroneously. Viewing and adjusting the figure within the Blue Channel enabled us to see it 'better' and therefore to record it better. Both manual and electronic drawing techniques can be combined with these image-enhancement techniques.

5 Drawing with Photoshop and manually

Photoshop can also be used to 'draw' images from scanned slides or photographs. 'Drawing' in Photoshop is different in that it involves selecting out a rock-art painting from its background rather than documenting it in a separate medium. A selection of slides from the region outlined below were drawn first in Photoshop and then manually. In assessing the software we posed these questions to ourselves: how does electronic drawing compare with manual drawing in terms of speed, quality, flexibility and permanence of the considered image arrived at? Should a rock-art researcher, interested in a good graphic record but not in computer work for its own sake, at this time continue with manual drawing, or switch partly or wholly to electronic methods? And how should we start to change our habits of drawing in light of the potential of the new electronic technologies?

6 The images

The rock-art images used in this study were photographed by one of us (CC) in tropical north Australia. The area from which they come is typical of the region, and typical of many rock-art areas, in offering a variety of paintings of varied ages and in varied states of preservation, with consequential varied issues arising in how best to draw them.

The earliest paintings, perhaps towards 5000 years old, include tiny, finely drawn silhouette human figures with high rounded headdresses. These are executed in an ochre that has faded greatly over time, often to a distinctively 'mulberry' hue. When they are much faded or when on rock with natural red staining, they are difficult to distinguish from the background support—a sandstone whose own tone often tends itself to pinkish or red. There are also large anthropomorphic figures with purple infills. The figures placed in the middle period are in bichrome, usually a reddish brown infill and a white outline; these seem a matter of hundreds of years old. The most recent phase of images consists of figures, still bright and fresh, in various combinations of whites, yellows, browns, greys, blues and reds.

These several groups of pictures differ in drawing style, pigment colour and levels of preservation, presenting a challenge to any graphics software package or manual recorder.

7 Equipment and procedures

The drawings were made from the field record existing as 35 mm slide photographs. All photography was in daylight using natural illumination. A conventional 35 mm SLR, Nikon F601 camera was used, generally with a 50 mm Nikon AF lens. Automatic focusing and exposure were generally used, with an exposure of 1/125 or 1/250 seconds. The film was Agfa Professional colour slide film, generally rated ASA 100 and 'pushed' one stop to be shot at ASA 200. It was processed using the standard E6 technique.

For electronic drawing we used an Apple Mac Power G3 with 160MB RAM running OS 8-1. The slides were scanned using a Polaroid Sprint Scan 35 at a resolution of 1350 d.p.i. This generates an image from a full 35 mm frame of about 1800 by 1250 lines per image, broadly comparable with a crisp colour photographic print of medium size. During the scan some minor adjustments in exposure and tonal range were made. The image files were then saved in the Adobe format, exported and opened in Adobe Photoshop. Images from many different sources (most notably, the Web) and saved in many different graphic formats can be opened in Photoshop.

Image resolution is a function of the number of pixels. A fairly crisp image on a computer monitor is typically 768 by 512 pixels, that is, about one-sixth of the number of pixels of these scans. But a 'fairly crisp' image on a screen is of a decidedly lower resolution than is expected of archive-quality archaeological recording, or of high-quality print reproduction.

After scanning in the slides, the rock-art images were selected out from their backgrounds. The selection was placed on a fresh layer, and that layer was printed out either in colour, in grayscale or in bitmap as a slide, as a photograph-quality print, or as a simple laser-print.

Photoshop offers several ways to select parts of an image including the 'Lasso', 'Marquee', 'Magic Wand' and 'Color Range' tools. Selection can be based on either image-edge recognition or colour recognition. After limited success with edge recognition techniques we decided to use the 'Color Range' command. This command selects a specified colour. The user can choose which colour is selected either from a menu bar in the Color Range dialogue box—options such as 'reds' or 'cyans'—or by selecting colours from the image itself. We have found the latter method more effective.

Within Photoshop it is simple to open a new layer and then to 'Copy', 'Cut' and 'Paste' your selection on to it. This layer can then have a scale added, be re-sized, be measured, have its volume quantified, have its resolution adjusted, and have text added. The new layer can be exported in a variety of ways—colour, grayscale, bitmap—to a variety of media—as a projection slide, by photo-quality printer, on a web-site, by laser-printer, or imported into other software programs.

In this case we first sample the dominant colour from the main body of the figure. The 'Color Range' command enables one to add or subtract other colours from the image; background tones can be selected out. The 'Fuzziness' box allows modification of the range of colours selected. If fuzziness is reduced, so too is the range of colour values selected.

This method works by selecting colour values, and those can be equated to pigment traces on the rock. It therefore provides an independent assessment of the shape of an image (see Figures 2 and 3). Methods based on manual tracing involve the user deciding where the edges of an image are, and can arguably be seen as more subjective.

Once an initial selection has been made using 'Color Range' it can be edited by hand by moving into a 'Quick Mask'. This mask allows the editing of a selection—both the adding and removing of parts—whilst the original image and your selection of it are simultaneously displayed. It is useful for checking the Photoshop selection against one's own interpretation of the figure. Combining the digital abilities of Photoshop with our own understanding of the image produced excellent results. Of course, hand editing reduces the objectivity of the result, if that is what one desires.

On faded images Photoshop can distinguish areas of faint colour, not so obvious to the unaided eye. However, because there was little colour differentiation between this figure and the rock surface, some hand editing was necessary (see Plate 3 and Figure 4).

Also of note in this recovery is the way in which Photoshop records the image not in a solid black hue but permits the pigment texture to be recorded.

In Photoshop it does prove harder to work with bichrome or polychrome images in which the colours used are very different from each other, for example red and white.

The Color Range command tends to select out too much of the image if both the colours are selected. This problem can be rectified by selecting out each colour independently, placing the selections on different layers and then merging these layers (see Figures 5 and 6) or by using edge-recognition techniques.

We see the images selected by Photoshop as being more accurate than those drawn by hand: they depend less on the viewer, being guided by colour values instead. The image produced is more realistic in that areas of doubt, damage or plain bad drawing are not 'corrected' by well-meaning researchers. In effect what this method produces is a structured photograph of the pigment remaining on the rock.

There is a steep learning curve involved in acquiring Photoshop skills. However, once these skills were acquired, we found that each image took about one hour to process.

8   Manual drawing

The same slides as used for the Photoshop experiment were reused. They were projected on to a light table and drawn on tracing paper in black ink. Each image took about two hours to record in this manner. If one starts with a field tracing and re-traces it in the lab, then it takes substantially longer.

When one draws manually, one records the edge of the line dividing the pigment from the ground (see Figure 7). As many field-workers will agree, this is not a simple task: what constitutes the edge of an image is not always apparent. There can be several interpretations of what a form is, particularly when—as is typical—the pigment has degraded and been partially lost. The first image drawn closely follows the edge of the pigment as it presently survives (Figure 8).

The second image smoothes the edges of the image and supposes to recover the form as originally

Figure 2: A white figure from the late phase, northern Australia. Reproduced by scanning a 35 mm slide and converting to grayscale.

Figure 3: A selection from the Figure 2 photograph made in Photoshop. The white-on-beige image was inverted to a black-on-white so that it was easier to see on the page.

Figure 4: A Photoshop selection from Plate 3 in grayscale.

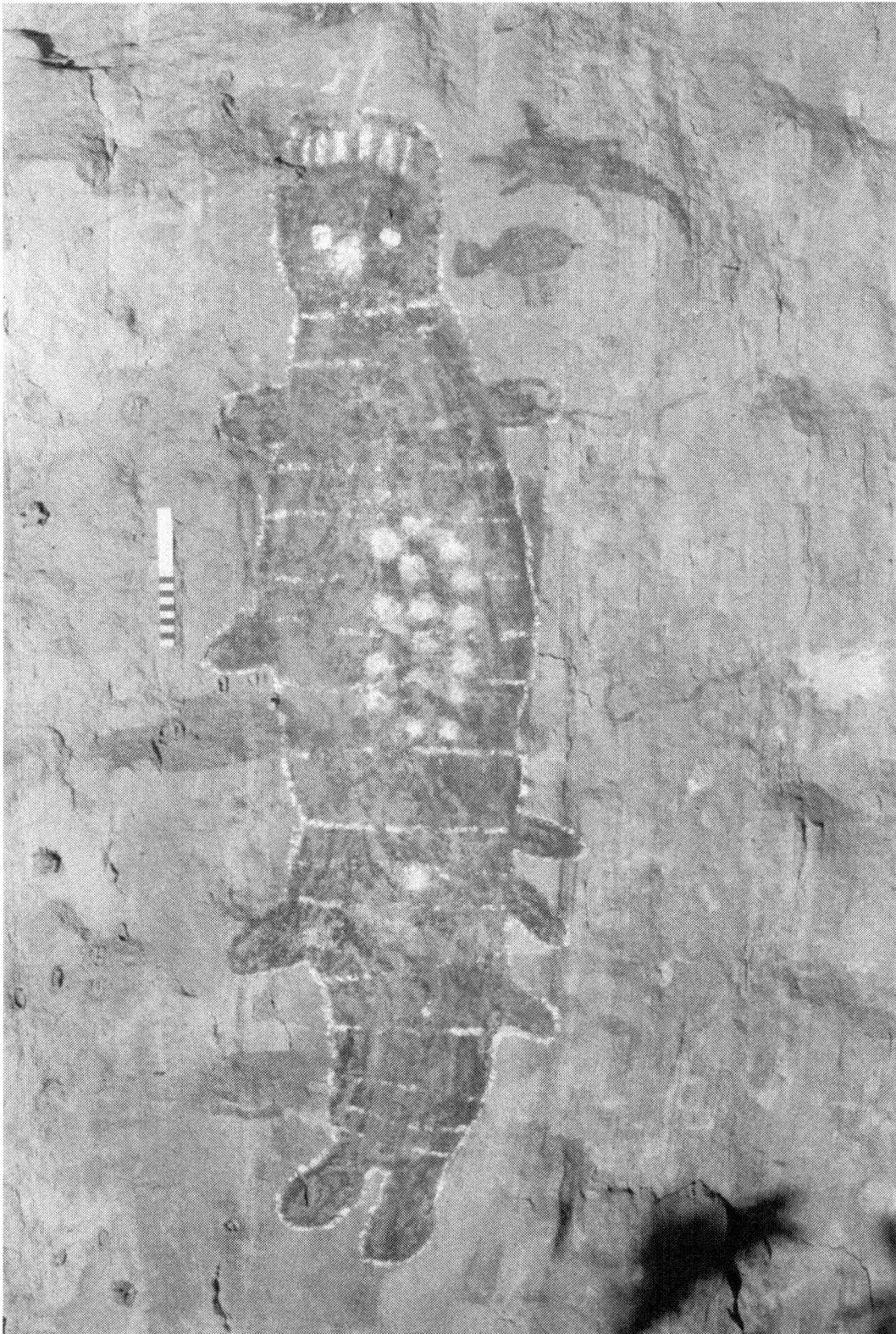

Figure 5: A photograph of a bichrome figure, northern Australia. Reproduced by scanning a 35 mm slide and converting to greyscale.

Figure 6: A Photoshop selection from Figure 5 in grayscale.

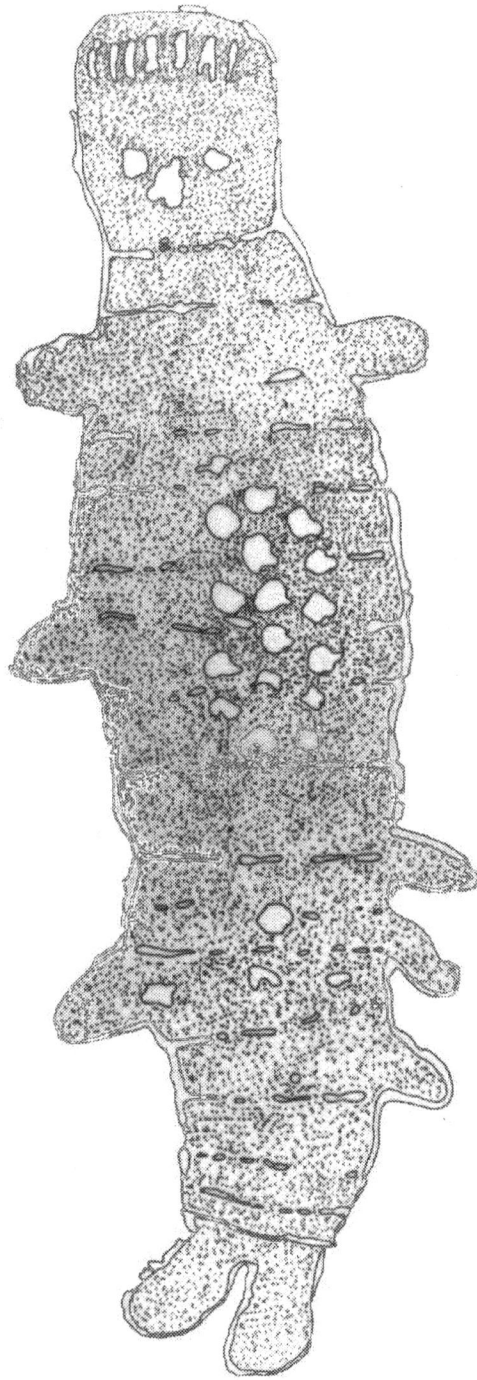

Figure 7: A hand-drawn image of Figure 5. Drawn from a projected 35 mm slide.

Figure 8: A hand-drawn outline of the figure in Plate 3.

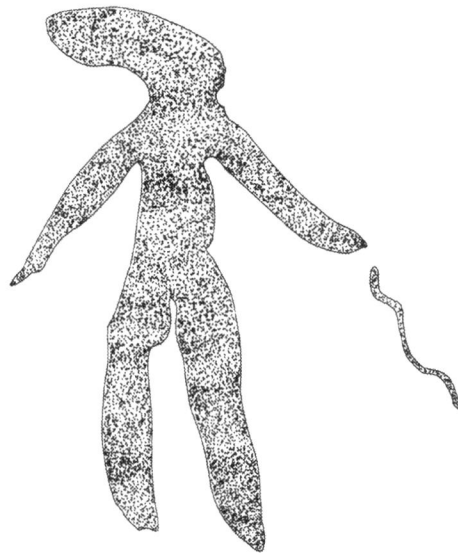

Figure 9: A hand-drawn interpretation of the figure in Plate 3.

Figure 10: A composite image of Figures 8 and 9 made in Photoshop.

made (Figure 9).

What does one choose? Fidelity to pigment as currently seen or a considered presentation of the original form as the researcher reasonably judges it to be? Here Photoshop can also be of use in enabling one to present both interpretations together (Figure 10).

Both tracings were scanned into Photoshop, re-scaled and mounted together to produce this interpretative panel. This practice also shows how, within Photoshop, images from different sources—manual drawings, photographs, computer-aided interpretations—can be combined and displayed together.

For those researchers who prefer manual techniques, it is worth noting that the presentation of hand-made images can be assisted by Photoshop. When outlines are scanned into the program they can easily be infilled using the 'Paintbucket' and other tools, faster than hand-filling. Quantitative measurements can be taken, the images can be re-scaled, and text can be added. A technique that we have not tried but of potential interest is the infilling of hand-drawn outlines with colours sampled from the original image; it is also possible to 'clone' pigment from the photographed original on to a hand-made outline giving it pigment texture as well as colour.

9 Discussion: electronic and manual drawing

In comparison with the coloured, textured images produced in Photoshop, these conventional drawings to us appear too formalized in their absolute contrast of black and white. The colour of the image and the real texture of the painting on the rock are lost. Through demanding an authoritative black line, publication conventions negate the real, dynamic existence of the paintings. With Photoshop many photographs of an image can be scanned in, compared, edited and summated, potentially by different researchers, allowing for multiple interpretations of a figure.

Photographs are neither objective nor always easy to understand: poor lighting conditions or bad photography may mean that the image scanned into Photoshop is less clear than seen on the rock with the eye, making it difficult to select from. Neither do photographs provide all the information required for the proper analysis of an image. The interpretation made of images during manual drawing does aid understanding. David Lewis-Williams makes the important point that drawing an image manually is part of the process of analysing and understanding that image. Areas of superimposition or other details are not always obvious on the first occasion that an image is examined. If these are in another colour, such details may be missed by Photoshop. If they are in a similar colour then the speed with which Photoshop will absorb these details within the main selection can mean that they could be missed. The closer examination of images that manual drawing requires, aids their analysis. As Lewis-Williams writes, 'Far from being an mechanical documentation of "facts", tracing is a form of analysis that is more than merely descriptive' (1990, 127). Further to this, manual drawings are clearer and are therefore better for illustrating or explaining panels, particularly to an inexperienced audience. A point also made by the Witwatersrand Rock Art Institute is that their manual interpretations are fairer to the original artists in that they re-capture the remarkable beauty of the art, not only its present-day form (B. Smith pers. comm.). Our comments must also be tempered by remembering the beautiful, full-colour painted reproductions done—manually—by some rock-art recorders (Vinnicombe 1976; Kirkland and Newcomb 1996; Battiss 1948; Pager 1975).

Concerning the more 'objective' nature of Photoshop-rendered images, it has been disputed whether a computer program can be called objective; in this case, the decisions made by the machine as to whether a certain colour is present or not depend upon its pre-programmed controlling algorithms (programmed by individuals). Further to this, the individual using Photoshop impacts their composition, design and use by setting thresholds (Leibhammer 1998; Shanks 1997; Sontag 1987; Gaffney and van Leusen 1995). These features suggest that we should be cautious in claiming an 'objective' label for Photoshop images: they are still products of a recording project initiated by humans and using human discrimination.

Although Photoshop is a program primarily intended for photographic work (hence its name), we refer here to 'electronic drawing' rather than 'electronic photography'. Why? Drawing always involves choice, judgement and convention in what is drawn and how: there are no 'givens'. Photography—at least for the inexperienced using one of the modern 'intelligent' cameras—has some appearance of being neutral or even objective. Working with electronic images can be approached in either spirit. We prefer to think in terms of drawing, because that approach emphasizes the element of choice and judgement. There are potential dangers in using a technique which allows part of an image or panel to be preferentially selected, enhanced or manipulated. The first use which Adobe's instruction manuals for Photoshop expect for its powerful tools is the adjusting of image colour and tone as colour *correction*; for our use, we prefer to think of colour *manipulation*, which only in some cases will hope to capture as close as can be done a certain 'natural' and 'correct' visual appearance. Our paper's referee remarks of our approach and our use of the word 'manipulation': 'Similarly, changing the way we visualize images should not be confused with changing our understanding of them.' We disagree: changing the way we visualize images *does* change our understanding of them. This is why electronic imaging, as photography did a century ago, will come fundamentally to change how we perceive rock-art and all archaeological materials.

What we have learnt from exploring these techniques of representation is that both methods produce good, if different results. As Photoshop does not understand art, it selects and defines areas by the colour of pigments, producing a record of the spatial arrangements of these. Arguably, this makes it a more objective recorder of rock-art. Manual drawing helps us to understand and present rock-art images. From that experience, like that of Andrea Arcà's project (Arcà 1998), we would recommend the use of multiple manual and computer-aided renditions of a rock surface so that its form is fully explored.

10 The consequences of using digital pathways

So far we, and most other researchers, when considering the role of graphic software in the analysis of rock-art, have had as our goal the optimal rendering of an image. Various programs have been used to help us 'see the image better' (Brayer *et al.* 1998; Clogg and Díaz-Andreu 1998; Arcà 1998). Understanding what an image is and recording it well are obviously vital steps in any investigation of a rock-art site (Lewis-Williams 1981); graphic software has great potential in this area. A more significant point, not discussed so far, is the impact that the use of these digital pathways will have on rock-art research. The use of new digital pathways, combined with electronic publishing techniques, have the potential to challenge the nature of rock-art research; digitization can open up new, different and challeng-

ing avenues of research, changing not only the way we draw, but the ways in which we question rock-art panels.

Digital image processing and publication in electronic media offer us a new way of 'seeing' rock-art. Seeing images differently opens up different questions (Bradley 1997a). Different ways of seeing have already opened up new areas of research in archaeology; thin-section analysis, magnetometer survey, theodolite and laser area plotting and—most notably—GIS have all changed the way in which a site is seen, how it is analysed and published (Leibhammer 1998). With the increasing use of electronic media in rock-art research, not only the way we visualize our sites but our research objectives will change too.

As became apparent in our comparison of the products of electronic and manual drawing, there may not be a single optimal rendering of an image. Different but equally valuable recordings can be made of the same image. Computer-aided images can challenge the authority of the 'single black line' by illustrating an image in varied ways. These multiple recordings of an image can also be published inexpensively in digitally based mediums. By moving away from a search for authoritative documentation we open rock-art up to new questions concerning visualization, subjectivity, multi-vocality and polysemy; all difficult issues but worth addressing.

Working in Photoshop allows us to present coloured, toned and textured rock-art images. Colour and texture are not issues that have been well addressed in rock-art research, perhaps because the constraints of black-and-white publishing make it impractical. Black-and-white publishing has led to an interest in 'black-and-white' questions, a situation that digitization has the potential to challenge. The frequently made and true statement that rock-painting is valuable because it remains in primary context can surely be complimented by the also true statement that rock-painting is valuable because it is made in colour. It is often one of the few vibrant elements of a otherwise largely mud-coloured past; as such it offers us a vital insight into that past. Digital pathways offer us the potential to use colour and to realize texture, opening up new areas of research and questioning.

Finally, working in a digital medium will make the collection and presentation of new kinds of data more feasible. By using complimentary software such as Live Picture's PhotoVista (see Table 1 for the URL) and Apple's QuickTime Virtual Reality (capable of merging together a se-

Web Resource	URL	Accessed
Apple	http://quicktime.apple.com	15/02/00
Live Picture	http://livepicture.com	9/3/00
Adobe Photoshop	http://www.adobe.com/products/photoshop/main.html	5/3/00

Table 1: URLs of Web resources cited in the text.

ries of digital photographs into a 'landscape' image and orienting the viewer within that image, see Table 1 for Apple's Web site) we will be better able to record and publish whole panels and to place these panels in a landscape. This may help us in addressing issues about form and its importance. Work on form and context are already being produced with interesting results (see Whitley 1998; Hartley and Wolley Vawser 1998; Skotnes 1994; Nettleton 1985; Smith 1994; Bradley 1997b); the application of digital methods could further enhance this field. The lodging of digital video of rock-art sites on Web pages could allow other researchers and interested parties to 'get a feel' for the often inaccessible sites too.

Publishing through electronic media will open our work to a far larger audience, thereby introducing more voices in rock-art research.

These briefly outlined ideas are not 'Startrek' speculations but real events occurring today; UNESCO is currently funding a project to digitize a complete complex rock-art site in Melanesia, the site of Çatalhöyük is also being digitized and published on the Web, electronic journals such as *Tracce*, are becoming available. A full digital recording of a rich rock-art site requires the types of resources that lie beyond most rock-art researchers but they do show (one of) the way(s) ahead. The average researcher can gain access to Photoshop; smaller-scale digitization, of even single images, presents rock-art information in a new and challenging way. The digital medium therefore is one that active researchers should familiarize themselves with.

pared and displayed. With the advent of new media technologies this flexibility will be of immense value.

Further to this, the images produced by electronic means are challenging to our definition of what a rock-art image should be like and indeed to what rock-art studies should be about. The use of digital techniques now lies within the budget and capabilities of most rock-art researchers and we are keen to see their potential fully explored by other researchers.

In a paper of a certain length, we have briefly addressed both some rather particular practicalities and some very general issues. Readers will notice rapid transitions between the two. Since rock-art is recorded and studied with a view to knowledge, and knowledge is disseminated through publication, the means of publication has an effect on all stages of work done before. The natural partner to electronic working with images is their electronic publication in the nascent formats of Internet and/or CD-ROM formats. To address those is beyond the scope of the present essay (see Chippindale 1999). The present essay is published in conventional printed technology in the established BAR format, which generally does not permit colour illustration, and whose printing specifications have consequences for image resolution (which then feed back into concerns of file size: see above). The editors and publisher kindly allowing us two pages of colour plates, we have used those to make two points concerning colour. For the rest we have emphasized aspects which can be sufficiently illustrated in monochrome illustration.

11   In conclusion

The use of graphics software and specifically of electronic drawing techniques, are of benefit to rock-art researchers. Coloured, textured images can be speedily produced and adjusted. Scales, text and quantifications can be simply added. Images can be imported from a variety of sources and likewise exported with great flexibility. Different image interpretations can be easily com-

12   Acknowledgements

We thank colleagues in Cambridge for advice about technical matters and colleagues in South Africa for guidance about rock-art recording. Emma Jane Read is funded by the British Academy and her fieldwork has been funded by Corpus Christi College, Cambridge University. Christopher Chippindale thanks a north Australian Aboriginal community for field access,

Australian National University and its North Australia Research Unit for field support, colleagues for field assistance; and acknowledges financial support from the Australian Institute of Aboriginal and Torres Strait Islander Studies and Cambridge University.

References

[1] Adobe 1998. *Adobe Photoshop 5.0: classroom in a book.* Adobe Systems, San Jose (CA).

[2] Adobe 1999. *Adobe Photoshop 5.5: classroom in a book.* Adobe Systems, San Jose (CA).

[3] Anati, E. 1994. *Valcamonica rock art: a new history for Europe.* Capo di Ponte, Edizioni del Centro.

[4] Arcà, A. 1998. Digital auto-tracing in rock art recording: applications of computer vectorial designs. *Tracce 11.* http://www.rupestre.net/tracce/tracce11.html, Accessed 9/3/00.

[5] Arcà, A. and Bulas Cruz, J. 1998. Rationale. *Tracce,* 11. http://www.rupestre.net/tracce/tracce11.html, Accessed 9/3/00.

[6] Battiss, W. W. 1948. *The artists of the rocks.* Pretoria, Red Fawn Press.

[7] Bednarik, R. G. and Seshadri, S. 1995. Digital colour re-construction in rock art photography. *Rock Art Research,* 12(1):24–52.

[8] Bégouën, R. and Clottes, J. 1987. Les Trois-frères after Breuil. *Antiquity,* 61:180–187.

[9] Bertani, D., Capanni, A., Cetica, M., Pezzati, L. and Pagliara, C. 1997. Digitised recording of petroglyphs in Poesia cave, Italy. *Rock Art Research,* 14(2):137–142.

[10] Bradley, R. 1997a. To see is to have seen: craft traditions in British field archaeology. In B. L. Molyneaux, (ed.), *The cultural life of images: visual representation in archaeology,* pp. 62–72. London, Routledge.

[11] Bradley, R. 1997b. *Signing the land: rock art and the prehistory of Atlantic Europe.* London, Routledge.

[12] Brayer, J. M., Walt, H. and David, B. 1998. Quantitative assessment of rock art recording. *Tracce,* 11. http://www.rupestre.net/tracce/tracce11.html, Accessed 9/3/00.

[13] Chippindale, C. 1999. The nature of data in paper and in electronic media. Paper presented at the Society for American Archaeology 64th annual meeting, Chicago (IL).

[14] Clegg, J. 1991. !Pictures and pictures of... In P. Bahn and A. Rosenfeld, (eds.), *Rock art and prehistory: papers presented to symposium G of the AURA Congress, Darwin 1988,* Oxbow Monograph 10, pp. 109–111, Oxford. Oxbow Books.

[15] Clogg, P. and Díaz-Andreu, M. 1998. Digital image processing and the recording of rock art. *Tracce,* 11. http://www.rupestre.net/tracce/tracce11.html, Accessed 9/3/00.

[16] Dickman, J. L. 1984. An image digitising and storage system for use in rock art research. *Rock Art Research,* 1(1):25–32.

[17] Donnan, E. 1998. Recording British rock art. *Tracce,* 11. http://www.rupestre.net/tracce/tracce11.html, Accessed 9/3/00.

[18] Evening, M. 2000. *Adobe Photoshop 5.5 for photographers: a professional image editor's guide to the creative use of Photoshop for the Macintosh and PC.* Oxford, Focal Press.

[19] Firnhaber, R. P. 1998. Printing digital images. *Tracce,* 11.

[20] Gaffney, V. and van Leusen, M. 1995. Postscript—GIS, environmental determinism and archaeology: a parallel text. In G. Lock and Z. Stancic, (eds.), *Archaeology and geographical information systems,* pp. 367–382. London, Taylor and Francis.

[21] Hartley, R. and Wolley Vawser, A. M. 1998. Spatial behaviour and learning in the prehistoric environment of the Colorado River drainage (south-eastern Utah), western North America. In C. Chippindale and P. S. C. Taon, (eds.), *The archaeology of rock-art,* pp. 373–384. Cambridge, Cambridge University Press.

[22] Henderson, J. W. 1995. An improved procedure for the photographic enhancement of rock paintings. *Rock Art Research,* 12(2):75–85.

[23] Kirkland, F. and Newcomb, W. W. 1996. *The rock art of the Texas Indians*. Austin (TX), University of Texas Press. Reissue of 1967. Kirkland (paintings) and Newcomb (text).

[24] Layton, R. 1991. Figure, motif and symbol in the hunter-gatherer rock art of Europe and Australia. In P. Bahn and A. Rosenfeld, (eds.), *Rock art and prehistory: papers presented to symposium G of the AURA Congress, Darwin 1988*, Oxbow Monograph 10, pp. 23–38, Oxford. Oxbow Books.

[25] Leibhammer, N. 1998. Visualising Çatalhöyük. Colloquium Papers 1 (unpublished).

[26] Lewis-Williams, J. D. 1981. *Believing and seeing: symbolic meanings in southern San rock paintings*. London, Academic Press.

[27] Lewis-Williams, J. D. 1990. Review article: documentation, analysis and interpretation, dilemmas in rock art research. *South African Archaeological Bulletin*, 152:126–136.

[28] Lewis-Williams, J. D. and Dowson, T. A. 1989. *Images of power: understanding Bushman rock art*. Johannesburg, Southern Book Publishers.

[29] Merrell, C. L. 1998. The application and evaluation of computer photo enhancement techniques for the documentation of petroglyphs and pictographs. Paper presented at the Society for American Archaeology 63rd annual meeting, Seattle (WA).

[30] Molyneaux, B. L. 1997. Introduction: the cultural life of images. In B. L. Molyneaux, (ed.), *The cultural life of images: visual representation in archaeology*, pp. 1–10. London, Routledge.

[31] Nettleton, A. 1985. The visual significance of southern San paintings. In *Conference papers from the Southern African Association of Art Historians 1985*, pp. 50–59.

[32] Pager, H. 1975. *Stone Age myth and magic*. Graz, Akademische Druck.

[33] RAPP 2000. *Rock Art Pilot Project: main report*. Bournemouth and London, Bournemouth University School of Conservation Sciences and University of London Institute of Archaeology for English Heritage.

[34] Rip, R. P. 1983. Digital recording and image processing of rock art by computer. *South African Archaeological Bulletin*, 38:77–79.

[35] Rip, R. P. 1989. Colour space transformations for the enhancement of rock art images by computer. *Rock Art Research*, 6(1):12–16.

[36] Sanger, K. K. and Meighan, C. W. 1990. *Discovering prehistoric rock art: a recording manual*. Calabasas (CA), Wormwood Press.

[37] Shanks, M. 1997. Photography and archaeology. In B. L. Molyneaux, (ed.), *The cultural life of images: visual representation in archaeology*, pp. 73–107. London, Routledge.

[38] Skotnes, P. 1994. The visual as a site of meaning. In T. A. Dowson and D. Lewis-Williams, (eds.), *Contested images: diversity in southern African rock art research*, pp. 315–329. Johannesburg, Witwatersrand University Press.

[39] Smith, A. B. 1994. Metaphors of space: rock art and territoriality in southern africa. In T. A. Dowson and D. Lewis-Williams, (eds.), *Contested images: diversity in southern African rock art research*, pp. 373–384. Johannesburg, Witwatersrand University Press.

[40] Sontag, S. 1987. *On photography*. London, Penguin Books.

[41] Tilley, C. 1991. *Material culture as text: the art of ambiguity*. London, Routledge.

[42] Vinnicombe, P. 1976. *People of the Eland: rock paintings of the Drakensberg Bushmen as a reflection of their life and thought*. Pietermaritzburg, University of Natal Press.

[43] Walt, H., David, B., Brayer, J. and Musello, C. 1997. International rock art database project. *Rock Art Research*, 14(1):44–50.

[44] Weinmann, E. and Lourekas, P. 1999. *Photoshop 5.5: for Windows and Macintosh*. Berkeley (CA).

[45] Whitley, D. S. 1998. Finding rain in the desert: landscape, gender and far western North American rock-art. In C. Chippindale and P. S. C. Taçon, (eds.), *The archaeology of rock-art*, pp. 185–211. Cambridge, Cambridge University Press.

Exploring archaeometric data using projection pursuit methodology

S. Westwood and M. J. Baxter

Department of Mathematics, Statistics and Operational Research
Clifton Campus, The Nottingham Trent University
Nottingham NG11 8NS, United Kingdom
email: simon.westwood@ntu.ac.uk

1 Introduction

Principal component analysis (PCA) is widely used in quantitative archaeological studies for investigating structure in multivariate data. It can be viewed as a particular application of projection pursuit (PP) methodology. The focus of this paper is on whether more general PP methods have much to offer in comparison to PCA for analyzing artefact compositional data in archaeometric studies.

Applications of multivariate methodology to chemical compositional data for artefacts, in the form of an $n \times p$ data matrix, $\mathbf{X}$, are among the most common uses of multivariate statistics in archaeology (Baxter 1994). Cluster analysis and PCA are the most widely used methods. The principal components, of which there are p, are uncorrelated linear combinations of the original variables. The first component has maximum variance, subject to a normalizing constraint on the coefficients; the second component has the second highest variance, and so on.

Results are often presented as plots based on the first few components, in the hope of revealing interesting structure in the data. Projection pursuit, as used here, might be similarly described, except that linear combinations of variables are sought which optimise an index other than variance and attempt, more directly, to measure 'interesting' structure in the data. It has been claimed that PCA is 'something of a blunt instrument' for detecting interesting structure because large variation need not be interestingly structured variation (Jones and Sibson 1987, 2).

Accessible methodological discussions of PP have been available in the British statistical literature since Jones and Sibson (1987), and in the Amer-

ican literature for somewhat longer (Friedman and Tukey 1974). Despite claims that applications of PP have 'flourished' (Posse 1995a, 84) and been 'promoted extensively in the literature and in implementation' (Nason 1995, 413), published practical applications—as opposed to theoretical papers—are quite hard to find. Flenley and Olbricht (1993) and Wilhelm *et al.* (1999) are the only applications to archaeological data that we know of, other than our own noted in the first example. Applications to data from other subject areas can be found in Friedman (1987), Jones and Sibson (1987), Nason (1995), Ripley (1996), Clements and Jones (1991), Glover and Hopke (1992, 1994), Lendzionowski *et al.* (1990) and Walden (1994). Several of these papers were written to explore the potential of PP in particular application areas, and this is the spirit in which this paper has been written.

Some of the theory of PP is discussed in the next section, along with practicalities of application. The heart of the paper is the third section, where a variety of applications are discussed. Our current thoughts on the usefulness of PP for archaeometric data analysis are presented in the final section.

2 Projection pursuit

2.1 Theory

Mathematical discussions are given in Huber (1985), Jones and Sibson (1987), Friedman (1987), Hall (1989), Cook *et al.* (1993), Sun (1991; 1993), Li and Cheng (1993), Eslava and Marriott (1994), Posse (1995a; 1995b) and Nason (1995), with a useful overview being provided by Ripley (1996, 296–303).

The central idea is to find k linear functions (projections) of the original variables that, when plotted, show interesting structure in the data. Usually $k = 1$ or $k = 2$ functions are sought, though $k = 3$ is possible (Nason 1995; Glover and Hopke 1992; 1994). Many approaches begin by equating *uninteresting* structure with the normal distribution and seek projections that are as non-normal as possible. For ease of exposition $k = 1$ is assumed in what follows.

Let $f(x)$ be the probability density of a random variable, X, with $\phi(x)$ the 'null' density when $f(x)$ has a normal distribution. A measure of weighted distance between $f(x)$ and the normal distribution is

$$I = \int (f(x) - \phi(x))^2 w(x)\, dx \qquad (1)$$

where $w(x)$ is a weight function. Equation 1 can be used as the basis for a variety of indices of interestingness; Cook *et al.* (1993) discuss indices for which $w(x) = \phi(x)^a$ for $a = -1$ (Friedman 1987), 0 (Hall 1989) and 1. Other forms of index are discussed in the references given above. Some of the indices that have been proposed for PP can be used as omnibus tests of normality (for example Mardia 1987) and Simonoff (1996, 117) has noted that any reasonable test statistic for normality is a candidate index.

For practical purposes $f(x)$ must be estimated. Using orthogonal series estimates of $f(x)$ and expansions of $\phi(x)$ Ripley (1996) notes that the index in equation 1 can be estimated as

$$\hat{I} = \sum_{i=0}^{\infty} w_i (a_i - b_i)^2 \qquad (2)$$

where a_i are the coefficients in the orthogonal series estimator; b_i are constants arising from the expansion for a normal distribution; and w_i depends on the weight function being used. For practical use the series in equation 2 must be truncated. Cook *et al.* (1993) call indices of the form given in equation 2 the *Legendre* (a = -1), *Hermite* (a = 0) and *Natural Hermite* (a = 1) indices after the orthogonal series expansions used to obtain the coefficients. Generalization to two-dimensional PP, of indices of the above type, is discussed in Cook *et al.* (1993) and Posse (1995a).

In the examples to follow we have used the two-dimensional Legendre, Natural Hermite and Friedman-Tukey indices, the last of which can be viewed as an estimate of the index $\int f(x)^2\, dx$ based on kernel density estimates (Jones and Sibson 1987, 5).

2.2 Practicalities

To implement two-dimensional projection pursuit the XGobi program (Swayne *et al.* 1991), which is freely available and can be run under X-Windows or from within the S-Plus package (Venables and Ripley 1997), has been used. The source of this, and other, software is discussed in the Appendix.

Many practitioners (for example Jones and Sibson 1987; Cook *et al.* 1993; Nason 1995) recommend 'sphering' the data before applying PP. This involves transforming the data to new variables that are uncorrelated and have the same variance. For most of our applications the data have been standardized to have zero mean and unit variance; principal components have been extracted; and the resultant principal component scores have been renormalized to have unit variance for each component. This results in a set of uncorrelated variables (essentially the principal components of standardized data) with equal variance. Some approaches to data analysis in archaeometry work routinely with logarithmically transformed but unstandardized data (for example Glascock 1992). It would be equally possible to sphere by finding the principal components of such data, and then renormalizing, though we have not used this approach below.

Typically p is in the range 8–30, but multicollinearity among the variables means that the effective dimensionality of the data is often much less than p. Typically more than 90% of the variation in the data will be accounted for by fewer than 10 principal components. The leading components, rather than the original variables, may be used in the PP.

A limitation of some approaches to PP is the sensitivity to outliers in the data, or to the tails rather than centre of the data. The moment index of Jones and Sibson (1987) has been criticised for the former reason (Ripley 1996, 300), and the Legendre index of Friedman (1987) for the latter reason (Cook *et al.* 1993, 228). It is possible to use PP as an informal method of multivariate outlier detection; if this is not of interest it is sensible to remove obvious outliers before analysis by PP, as they will often be the dominant feature of 'interesting' projections.

Sample size may also be a practical problem. Cook *et al.* (1993, 244–5) provide examples to show that for sparse, high-dimensional data PP can suggest spurious structure in random data. One of their cautionary examples shows apparent structure in a 100×5 data set, generated randomly from a normal distribution. Many archaeometric data sets have smaller n and larger p, so that particular heed should be paid to their warning that 'exploratory projection pursuit will always find structure, albeit weak, but care must be taken when emphasizing the significance of that structure'. In similar vein Ripley (1996, 301) suggests that, with large p PP 'may be used for hypothesis formation, but we will need independent evidence of the validity of the structure suggested by the plots'.

In the indices that have been discussed z, in the one-dimensional case, is a linear combination of p variables. The coefficients of this linear combination must be estimated and this leads to a non-linear optimisation problem in p dimensions which must be solved numerically. For higher dimensions the problem is obviously compounded. In XGobi the optimisation can be tracked, and numerous local optima will be found that may correspond to interesting views of the data. This will be illustrated in our second example. The ability of PP to produce multiple views of the data is widely seen as an attraction of the method as will be discussed in the final section, but is also time consuming.

Ripley (1996) observes that there is no unanimity in practice about which indices to use and advises that several should be tried. This has been done here, and the examples that follow represent only a small selection of the analyses that have been undertaken.

3 Examples

3.1 Example 1 - Lead isotope data

The following example, based on Baxter (1999), will be discussed in summary form only. We have used the method to be presented routinely in past work, but have not previously noted its interpretation as a PP method. Lead isotope ratio data are three-dimensional and in their analysis it has sometimes been assumed that data from an ore source can be treated as a sample from a multivariate normal distribution (Sayre *et al.* 1992). Recent work by Baxter and Gale (1998) and Baxter (1999) has called into question the general validity of this assumption. In particular, Baxter (1999) used a variety of tests of multivariate normality to demonstrate that many of the data sets in Stos-Gale *et al.* (1996) could not reasonably be regarded as samples from normally distributed data.

One test used was the multivariate extension of the univariate Shapiro-Wilk test statistic for normality (Malkovich and Afifi 1973). In this test the linear combination of the three lead isotope ratios is sought that minimizes the univariate statistic. This can be viewed as a PP method that results in a linear function, $k = 1$, that best displays the non-normality of the data. Figure 1 shows a kernel density estimate of the most non-normal linear combination for the Kea field, with $n = 62$. Formal tests of normality suggest that the data are non-normal and this particular application of PP methodology suggests that the data are strongly multi-modal. Further illustrations of this kind of use can be found in Baxter and Gale (1998) and Baxter (1999).

3.2 Example 2 - Blue soda glass from York

Cox and Gillies (1986) published analyses of blue soda glass from the windows of York Minster and archaeological excavations that has been used elsewhere to illustrate a variety of methodologies (Baxter 1989; Baxter and Buck 2000; Bell and Croson 1998). There are 27 specimens, measured with respect to the concentration of 12 oxides and elements. Most analyses clearly show three main groups in the data, with some analyses suggesting possible sub-groups or outliers.

Figure 2 shows four analyses of the data. The PCA analysis (of standardized data) in Figure 2(a) shows the three groups, one of which is dispersed relative to the other two. This structure is readily found using PP, and an example is given in Figure 2(b), where the structure is even more apparent. The view illustrated in Figure 2(c), in which the structure is 'circular', occurs quite commonly in our experience with similar data sets, and has no useful practical interpretation. Similar examples can be found in Cook *et al.* (1993, 248) and Ripley (1996, 302). Figure 2(d) shows a view in which outliers are the predominant feature.

We may remark that for this data set the structure is fairly obvious and found almost 'instantaneously' by PCA. Other useful views were not found in the course of exploration using PP. The PP view in Figure 2(b) is 'sharper' than the PCA view, but tells essentially the same story.

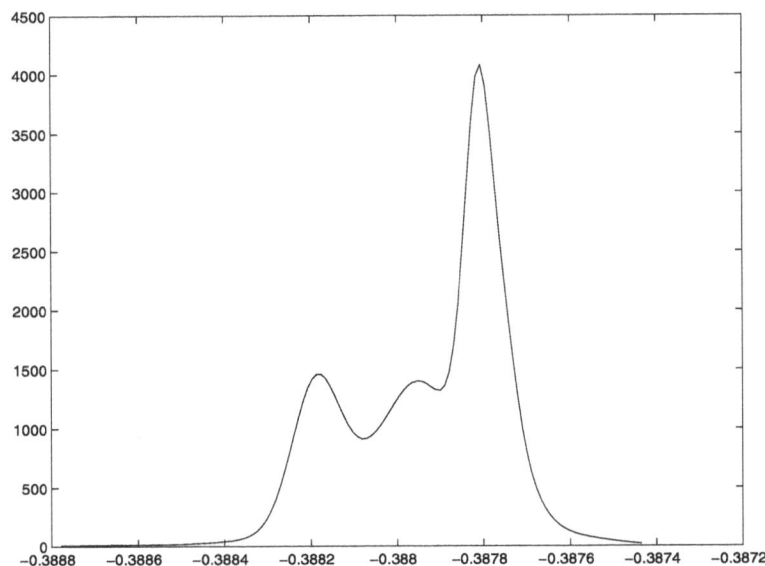

Figure 1: A kernel density estimate of the most non-normal linear combination of three-dimensional lead isotope ratio data for the Kea field.

3.3 Example 3 - Waste glass from Leicester and Mancetter

The data used in this example consist of 105 specimens of waste glass found on furnace sites at Leicester and Mancetter and measured with respect to the concentration of 11 major and minor oxides. It is of interest to see if there are distinct chemical groups in the data, and if these correspond to the furnace sites. The data were collected and published by Jackson (1992) and are reproduced in Baxter (1994) where extensive analysis was undertaken using a variety of multivariate methods. These analyses suggest three concentrations in the data with some correspondence—by no means exact—to the furnace groups.

This is shown in the PCA plot in Figure 3(a), where labelling is by site. Without a knowledge of the sites it is possible, visually or with the aid of techniques such as kernel density estimation (Baxter *et al.* 1997) to detect three main concentrations in the data. There are no obviously distinct clusters. The densest concentration to the right consists mainly of glass from Leicester; the other two concentrations contain most of the Mancetter specimens, with 11 to 14 Leicester specimens mixed in (depending on how boundaries of concentrations are visualised).

The PP view in Figure 3(b) quite clearly isolates a cluster of cases in the bottom half of the plot consisting, with one exception, of Leicester specimens. The remaining dispersed group, possibly sub-dividing into two, contains the Mancetter specimens with the same number of Leicester specimens mixed in as in the PCA.

Arguably the PCA and PP analyses lead to similar conclusions, but the separation between material from the two sites, and the fact that it is less than perfect, is clearer in the latter analysis because of the clearer clustering revealed. We remark that we can be confident that PP is not revealing spurious structure in this case because information not used in the PP, concerning site of origin, allows us to interpret the revealed structure in a useful archaeological manner.

3.4 Example 4 - Oriental Greenwares

This example is based on a 133×9 data set published by Pollard and Hatcher (1986) showing the chemical composition of 133 oriental greenwares which are suspected to have originated from several areas of manufacture. We follow them in omitting three clear outliers and one variable, SiO_2, in our analysis.

There are two very obvious chemical groups in the data, as the PCA in Figure 4(a) shows. The group to the left is associated with Northern Zhejiang Yue wares and that to the right with Longquan celadons. It is easy to get the same separation using PP and one such view is shown in the Figure 4(b). This additionally suggests a small group at the bottom of the plot that is a subset of the earlier wares, but we have been un-

84

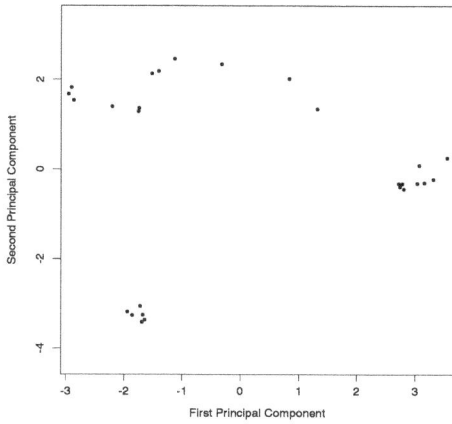

(a) PCA of standardised data

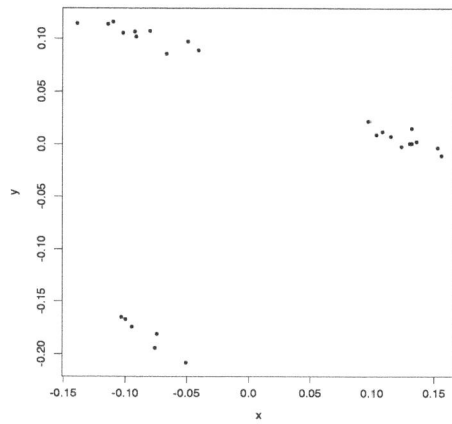

(b) PP using Friedman-Tukey index

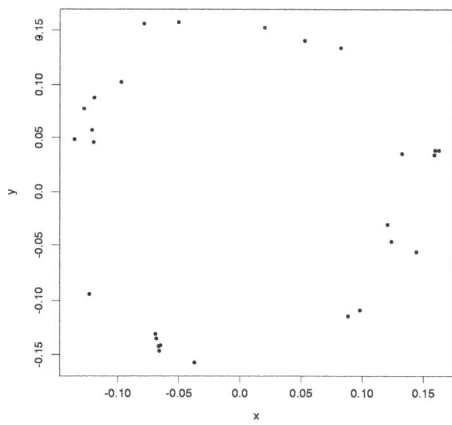

(c) PP using Natural Hermite index

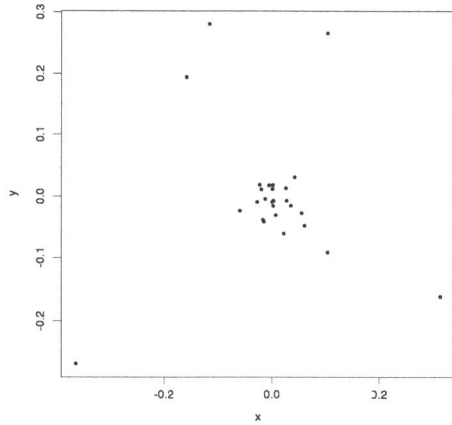

(d) PP using Natural Hermite index

Figure 2: Plots of York Minster data.

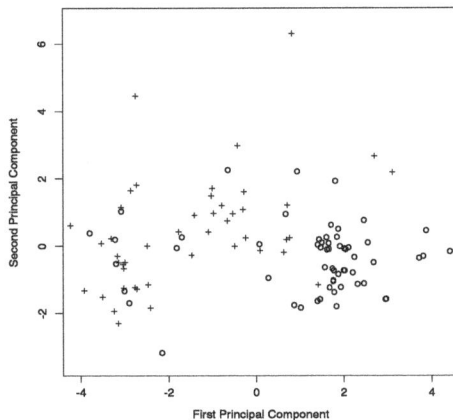

(a) PCA of standardised data

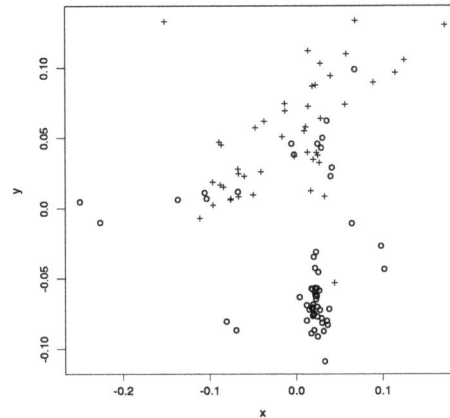

(b) PP using Legendre index

Figure 3: Plots based on analyses of the waste glass compositions from Mancetter and Leicester. Labelling is by site with '+' cases from Mancetter and 'o' cases from Leicester.

able to interpret this as archaeologically distinct in any way.

Pollard and Hatcher (1986) applied cluster analysis to the 53 specimens in the earlier group and concluded there were three subgroups. After applying stepwise discriminant analysis to these, five outliers were removed and a discriminant analysis plot for the remaining 48 cases was shown on page 268 of their paper. A similar analysis is shown in Figure 4(c), the only difference being our use of all eight variables rather than the five selected in the original publication. Interpretation of the groups is not absolutely clear-cut, but they can be associated with regional differences in composition. Given a knowledge of this classification we have been unable to obtain a PP view that separates out the groups as well as the discriminant analysis. In Figure 4(d) one PP view for the 48 cases is shown which separates out the smaller group but not the two larger ones. It may be noted that a PCA analysis of this subset (not shown) did as well as the PP in separating the groups.

Our PP analysis of this data set cannot be regarded as especially successful. Although the PP for the full data set did suggest structure additional to that revealed by PCA we were unable to interpret the results in an archaeologically useful fashion, so have no real way of determining whether the structure is spurious or not. Similar remarks apply to other PP analyses of the subset used in Figure 4 that are not shown here.

4 Discussion

For the specialized problem of Example 1 there is no doubt that one-dimensional PP, as illustrated there, has a useful role to play. Our current practice is to use PP in conjunction with tests of normality to explore the nature of the non-normality when it occurs. Unpublished work in progress suggests that the use of PP in isolation can mislead if the sample sizes are small.

Examples 2 and 3, particularly the latter, show that two-dimensional PP can produce a sharper view of structure in the data than that provided by PCA, but it was also the case that PP did not lead to an interpretation different from that achieved with PCA. In example 4 the PP analysis did not lead to any new insights into the data. Although some additional structure was suggested there is no obvious way of determining whether it is spurious or not. Our experience with these data sets is representative of others we have worked with.

In the wider literature there undoubtedly exist examples where PP does produce informative views of the data that PCA does not reveal. This sometimes occurs when the structure in the data is 'unusual' (see, for example, the structures used in Posse's (1995a, 91) simulation study), and of a kind that we suspect would often be regarded as uninterpretable in the context of the type of data used here. The model, often implicit, in studies that produce data similar to those used in exam-

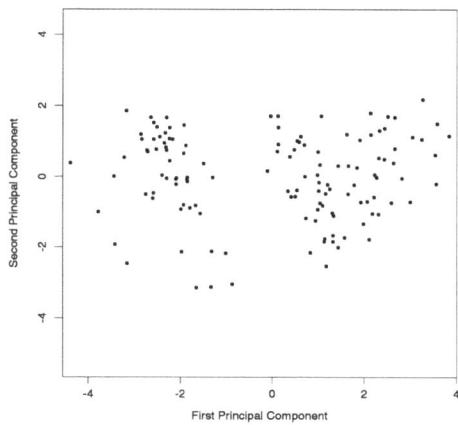

(a) PCA of standardised data

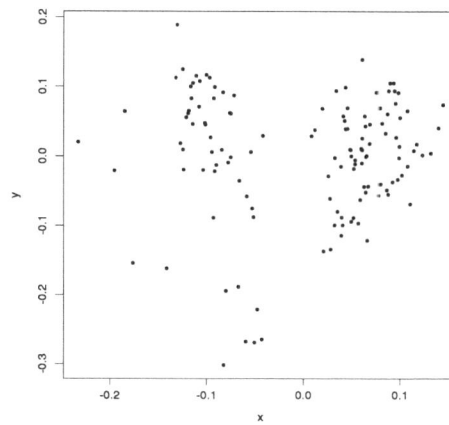

(b) PP using Friedman-Tukey index

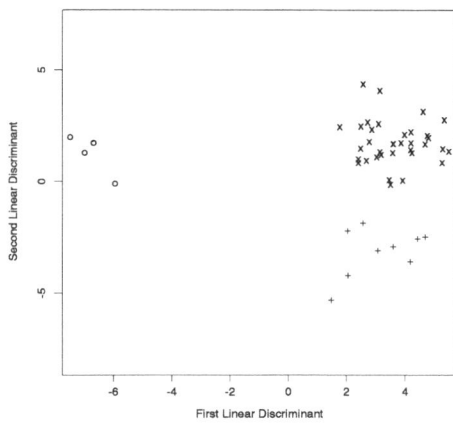

(c) Discriminant analysis plot for the smaller group from Figure 4(a)

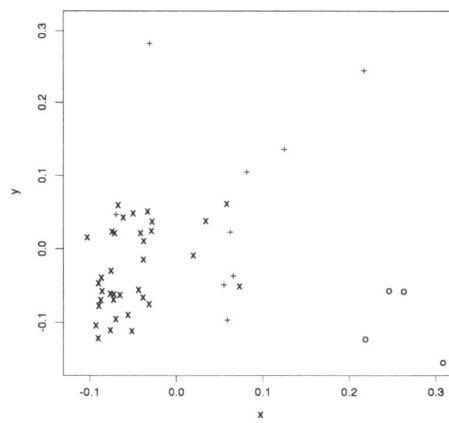

(d) PP using Legendre index for the smaller group from Figure 4(a)

Figure 4: Plots based on analyses of the oriental Greenware compositions. Figures 4(c) and 4(d) use data from the left-hand group showing in Figure 4(a), after omitting five outliers, labelled according to the groups determined by Pollard and Hatcher (1986).

Label in Appendix	URL for software	Accessed
1	http://www.research.att.com/~andreas/xgobi/	21/02/00
2	http://www.stats.ox.ac.uk/pub/SWin/xgobi.zip	21/02/00
3	http://lib.stat.cmu.edu/general/projpurs	21/02/00
4	http://www.stats.bris.ac.uk/~guy/Research/PP/PP.html	21/02/00
5	http://www.stats.bris.ac.uk/pub/software/pp2/mcj_pp.shar.gz	21/02/00

Table 1: Freely available projection pursuit software

ples 2, 3 and 4 is that the data may be viewed as a sample from a mixture of distributions which, in those studies that make statistical assumptions, are multivariate normal. In p-dimensional space the expectation is either that there will be distinct point clouds, or that there will be overlapping point clouds with distinct high-density regions. We suspect that methods such as PCA or cluster analysis will often be adequate to detect this, and that a PP view showing a marked departure from the underlying model might be difficult to interpret (we also recognise that this is not a good argument for not using PP).

Where PP has been contrasted with PCA and judged to be superior (for example Glover and Hopke 1992) the judgement is sometimes a fine one. It is also the case that in order to select a PP view and judge that it is superior to PCA it may be necessary to use additional information (for example a prior classification of the data) to confirm that the PP view is a useful one. Given the ease with which PP can suggest spurious structure with 'small' data sets we have found it very difficult to interpret results where such prior knowledge has not been available. The superiority of PP compared with PCA has sometimes been exaggerated. Posse (1995a, 83–84) analyses data on five measurements for 200 Australian crabs, most belonging to four groups. He claims that PP is able to reveal a 'clustered projection' that was 'not found by principal component analysis'. In fact the first component has an obvious size interpretation, and any of several standard approaches to PCA that aim to remove size effects (including a plot of the second and third components) will reveal a clustered projection similar to that found by PP.

Thus, while not disputing the theoretical interest of PP or its potential for revealing unusual and unexpected structure in large data sets, we remain agnostic about its value as a tool for the *routine* analysis of data of the kind discussed in examples 2–4. In addition to the reasons discussed so far, there are two pragmatic reasons that give rise to this agnosticism. The first concerns the size of the data sets typically available. Most examples of two-dimensional PP that we have seen use $p < 10$; our examples used $p = 8$, 11 and 12; it is now quite common to see analyses based on data sets for which $p > 20$. There has not been a commensurate increase in the size of samples typically collected, so that $n < 100$ is quite usual. In the context of a technique that can easily suggest spurious structure in small data sets, and where 100×5 is considered to be small (Cook *et al.* 1993), many archaeometric data sets are small and subject to the problems that this entails.

Our second reason concerns the time required to carry out PP. A large number of local optima arise in analysis, and the views they are associated with need to be inspected to see if they are 'interesting' and have a useful archaeological interpretation. In XGobi the plots produced in the course of pursuit can be viewed in real time and visually 'interesting' projections, including some used here, do not necessarily even correspond to local optima. These also need to be assessed and this is very demanding of time and has not, in the many analyses that we have undertaken, led to much extra insight into the data being gained, beyond that provided by PCA and cluster analysis—the tools most usually deployed in the literature. For these and other reasons we do not view PP, in its current state of development, as a tool we would recommend for routine archaeometric data analysis.

Appendix - Software availability

Freely available projection pursuit software is listed in Table 1. The software used in this paper was obtained from the first of the listed sites. Other sources of PP software are also listed, but we should stress that we have no experience in using these.

The XGobi software we used, running under X-Windows, is freely available and may be obtained from source 1 in Table 1. A Microsoft Windows version can be found at 2. FORTRAN software for two-dimensional PP (Friedman, 1987) can be found at 3 and 4 where software for Nason's (1995) three-dimensional PP is also available. FORTRAN code for two-dimensional PP from Jones and Sibson (1987) can be found at 5.

Acknowledgements

We are grateful to Nick Fieller for drawing our attention to some previous archaeological applications of projection pursuit.

References

[1] Baxter, M. J. 1989. Multivariate analysis of data on glass compositions: a methodological note. *Archaeometry*, 31:45–53.

[2] Baxter, M. J. 1994. *Exploratory Multivariate Analysis in Archaeology*. Edinburgh, Edinburgh University Press.

[3] Baxter, M. J. 1999. On the multivariate normality of lead isotope fields. *Journal of Archaeological Science*, 26:117–124.

[4] Baxter, M. J., Beardah, C. C. and Wright, R. V. S. 1997. Kernel density estimation for archaeology. *Journal of Archaeological Science*, 24:347–354.

[5] Baxter, M. J. and Buck, C. E. 2000. Data handling and statistical analysis. In E. Ciliberto and G. Spoto, (eds.), *Modern Analytical Methods in Art and Archaeology*. New York (in press), Wiley.

[6] Baxter, M. J. and Gale, N. H. 1998. Testing for multivariate normality via univariate tests: a case study using lead isotope ratio data. *Journal of Applied Statistics*, 25:679–691.

[7] Bell, S. and Croson, C. 1998. Artificial neural networks as a tool for archaeological data analysis. *Archaeometry*, 40:139–151.

[8] Clements, A. M. and Jones, M. C. 1991. An ecological example of the application of projection pursuit to compositional data. *Vegetatio*, 95:101–117.

[9] Cook, D., Buja, A. and Cabrera, J. 1993. Projection pursuit indexes based on orthonormal function expansions. *Journal of Computational and Graphical Statistics*, 2:225–250.

[10] Cox, G. A. and Gillies, K. J. S. 1986. The X-ray fluorescence analysis of medieval durable blue soda glass from York Minster. *Archaeometry*, 28:57–68.

[11] Eslava, G. and Marriott, F. H. C. 1994. Some criteria for projection pursuit. *Statistics and Computing*, 4:13–20.

[12] Flenley, E. C. and Olbricht, W. 1993. Classification of archaeological sands by particle size analysis. In O. Opitz, B. Lausen and R. Klar, (eds.), *Information and Classification. Concepts, Methods and Applications. Proceedings of the 16th Annual Conference of the Gesellschaft fr Klassifikation e. V.*, pp. 478–489. Berlin, Heidelberg, Springer.

[13] Friedman, J. H. 1987. Exploratory projection pursuit. *Journal of the American Statistical Association*, 82:249–266.

[14] Friedman, J. H. and Tukey, J. W. 1974. A projection pursuit algorithm for exploratory data analysis. *IEEE Transactions on Computers*, 23:881–889.

[15] Glascock, M. D. 1992. Characterization of archaeological ceramics at MURR by neutron activation analysis and multivariate statistics. In H. Neff, (ed.), *Chemical Characterization of Ceramic Pastes in Archaeology*, pp. 11–26. Madison, Wisconsin, Prehistory Press.

[16] Glover, D. M. and Hopke, P. K. 1992. Exploration of multivariate chemical data by projection pursuit. *Chemometrics and Intelligent Laboratory Systems*, 16:45–59.

[17] Glover, D. M. and Hopke, P. K. 1994. Exploration of multivariate atmospheric particulate compositional data by projection pursuit. *Atmospheric Environment*, 28:1411–1424.

[18] Hall, P. 1989. Polynomial projection pursuit. *The Annals of Statistics*, 17:589–605.

[19] Huber, P. J. 1985. Projection pursuit (with discussion). *Annals of Statistics*, 13:435–525.

[20] Jackson, C. M. 1992. *A Compositional Analysis of Roman and Early Post-Roman Glass and Glass-working Waste from Selected British Sites*. PhD thesis, University of Bradford, UK.

[21] Jones, M. C. and Sibson, R. 1987. What is projection pursuit? (with discussion). *Journal of the Royal Statistical Society A*, 150:1–36.

[22] Lendzionowski, V., Walden, A. T. and White, R. E. 1990. Seismic character mapping over resevoir intervals. *Geographical Prospecting*, 38:951–969.

[23] Li, G. Y. and Cheng, P. 1993. Some recent developments in projection pursuit in China. *Statistica Sinica*, 3:35–51.

[24] Malkovich, J. F. and Afifi, A. A. 1973. On tests for multivariate normality. *Journal of the American Statistical Association*, 68:176–179.

[25] Mardia, K. V. 1987. Discussion of 'What is projection pursuit?' by Jones and Sibson (1987). *Journal of the Royal Statistical Society A*, 150:22–23.

[26] Nason, G. P. 1995. Three-dimensional projection pursuit. *Applied Statistics*, 44:411–430.

[27] Pollard, A. M. and Hatcher, H. 1986. The chemical analysis of oriental ceramic body compositions: part 2 - greenwares. *Journal of Archaeological Science*, 13:261–287.

[28] Posse, C. 1995a. Tools for two-dimensional exploratory projection pursuit. *Journal of Computational and Graphical Statistics*, 4:83–100.

[29] Posse, C. 1995b. Projection pursuit exploratory data analysis. *Computational Statistics and Data Analysis*, 20:669–687.

[30] Ripley, B. D. 1996. *Pattern Recognition and Neural Networks*. Cambridge, UK, Cambridge University Press.

[31] Sayre, E. V., Yener, K. A., Joel, E. C. and Barnes, I. L. 1992. Statistical evaluation of the presently accumulated lead isotope data from anatolia and surrounding regions. *Archaeometry*, 34:73–105.

[32] Simonoff, J. S. 1996. *Smoothing Methods in Statistics*. New York, Springer.

[33] Stos-Gale, Z. A., Gale, N. H. and Annetts, N. 1996. Lead isotope data from the Isotrace laboratory, Oxford *Archaeometry* data base 3, ores from the Aegean, part 1. *Archaeometry*, 38:381–390.

[34] Sun, J. 1991. Significance levels in exploratory projection pursuit. *Biometrika*, 78:759–769.

[35] Sun, J. 1993. Some practical aspects of exploratory projection pursuit. *SIAM Journal on Scientific Computing*, 14:68–80.

[36] Swayne, D. F., Cook, D. and Buja, A. 1991. *User's manual for XGobi, a dynamic graphics program for data analysis implemented in the X Windows system (Release 2)*. Bellcore Technical Memorandum.

[37] Venables, W. N. and Ripley, B. D. 1997. *Modern Applied Statistics with S-Plus: Second Edition*. New York, Springer.

[38] Walden, A. T. 1994. Spatial clustering: using simple summaries of seismic data to find the edge of an oil-field. *Applied Statistics*, 43:385–398.

[39] Wilhelm, A. F. X., Wegman, E. J. and Symanzik, J. 1999. Visual clustering and classification: The Oronsay particle size data set revisited. *Computational Statistics*, 14:109–146.

Beyond significant patterning, towards past intentions: the location of Orcadian chambered tombs

Patricia E. Woodman

Department of Continuing Education
University of Reading, London Road
Reading, RG1 5AQ, United Kingdom
email: P.E.Woodman@rdg.ac.uk

1 Introduction

1.1 Methodological background

Geographic Information Systems (GIS) have been widely adopted within many spheres of archaeology and there is a steadily growing body of literature on the topic. The last decade and a half has seen the archaeological community follow rather a roller-coaster path in its regard for GIS. At the outset it was regarded as the perfect methodology and framework for 'doing' archaeology. This is typified by many of the contributions to the volume *Interpreting Space: GIS and Archaeology* (Allen *et al.* 1990). Notable examples include Green 1990, Savage 1990, Zubrow 1990, Warren 1990, Crumley and Marquardt 1990, Hasenstab and Resnick 1990, and Allen 1990. This was followed by the warnings and accusations that the use of GIS risked restricting the general development of archaeological thought and encouraging environmentally, functionally and technologically determinist analytical viewpoints (Gaffney *et al.* 1995, 211; Gaffney and van Leusen 1995, 372; Harris and Lock 1995, 354–5). However the latest trend has been to move toward using GIS to model perception and cognition within the past landscapes (Gaffney *et al.* 1995; Gaffney *et al.* 1996; Llobera 1996; Ruggles and Medyckyj-Scott 1996; Wheatley 1996).

Throughout the roller-coaster journey there has been a reoccurring issue of how to identify causation as opposed to mere correlation in the archaeological record (Wheatley 1995, 180; 1996; Maschner 1996a, 8; van Leusen 1998). GIS is adept at helping to identify patterns in the data, but it is in attributing meaning to (and even the intention behind) the patterning that we must now make advances. This paper reports on work that aims to employ GIS to explore the possible intentions that lay behind the location of Orcadian Neolithic burial monuments.

1.2 Archaeological background

The Orcadian Neolithic tombs have attracted the attention of researchers since the nineteenth century, when they were termed 'Picts' houses' (Petrie 1863). The development of the study of these monuments is well-documented (Davidson and Henshall 1989, 6–8) and does not need to be repeated here. Suffice to say that as a group of extant monuments the Orcadian chambered tombs have been the subject of intensive study from many different perspectives (Childe 1942; 1952; 1956; Ritchie 1959; Renfrew 1973; 1979; Hodder 1982; Hedges 1983; Fraser 1988; Davidson and Henshall 1989). A recurring theme of past research is the question of why tombs are located where they are.

Over the years researchers have made various observations concerning the distribution pattern of the Orcadian Chambered tombs and on possible influences on location. The distribution of sites on the island of Rousay has been a particular focus of study. Childe (1942) noted the correlation between the distribution of chambered cairns and 19th century settlement pattern and the township areas. Renfrew (1973, 149–50; 1979) developed this further using Thiessen polygons to delineate territories associated with each of the known cairns on the island of Rousay. Childe had also noted that the cairns were located on either modern or recently cultivated land or on the border between arable and heath land. He inferred from this that proximity to agricultural land was a determining factor in their location (1942, 141).

However analysis by Davidson (1979, 18) suggested that better agricultural soils were not correlated with the cairn distribution, rather he felt that easy access to the sea, the presence of steep and high land and the occupation of a commanding position were the influential factors on location. Fraser (1983, 269–87 and 263–9) noted correlations between cairn locations and well drained soils and sources of building stone. Davidson (1979, 13–14) also noted the correlation between the area visible from the tombs and the areas of land under cultivation today, which significantly includes the main clusters of modern settlements. He suggests that the cairns were built in prominent situations and that the main zone of activity for each group on the island was within sight of their cairn.

Since Davidson's work in the 1970s, it has frequently been noted that the Orcadian chambered tombs are located at 'prominent' places in the landscape. And a number of studies have been carried out concerning visibility and location of the tombs. Various observations can be found in the literature.

Davidson and Henshall (1989, 15) note that 'a striking feature to the fieldworker is the prominence of the actual sites on which cairns have been built'. They also say that 'the cairns are certainly conspicuous but give the impression of being sited to overlook a certain area' (Davidson and Henshall 1989, 17). Davidson and Henshall (1989) refer to Fraser's 1983 work saying that it demonstrates that there seems to have been a 'preference for siting cairns with wide areas of intermediate visibility, but that sites with restricted views were definitely avoided' (Davidson and Henshall 1989, 17). Fraser himself can be quoted as saying, 'unequivocally, certain types of visibility were part of the selection procedure in the location decision of the cairn-builders' (Fraser 1988).

Such observations clearly indicate some patterning in the location of tombs with prominence and visibility. However these comments are often the result of subjective (personal observation), qualitative (rather than quantitative), and sometimes partial observation (much of the work has concentrated on the Rousay cairns alone). Is there really a true pattern for all the known sites in Orkney? If so, can we be any more specific about what the pattern really is? What does it actually mean? Why were they located in such positions?

The above comments extracted from previous research demonstrate that visibility was of importance in relation to tomb location, but in what way? Were they positioned *to be* visible, or to *view from*? We could extend this to ask, were they positioned for the benefit of the living or the dead? In other words were tombs located to be visible to the community as they went about their daily activities or where they located to, perhaps, give the ancestral spirits a vantage point from which to keep watch or to begin their journey to the next life?

This paper will attempt to explore questions concerning the motivation behind tomb location using viewshed analysis as a means of quantifying the precise nature of the 'visibility' that exists and thus gain an insight into the Prehistoric rational behind tomb siting.

2 Viewshed analysis

Viewshed analysis is the process by which it is possible to simulate the area of landscape visible from a given point, within a specified distance. In practice the landscape is broken down into a grid of regular cells and a line-of-sight algorithm is used to test whether any cell within the specified radius is blocked from view by a nearer cell with a higher elevation.

Viewshed analysis has already received much attention from archaeologists. In a recent paper van Leusen (1998) reviewed the development of viewshed analysis in archaeology, citing applications ranging from their use in cultural resource management for carrying out visual impact analysis tests, to studies on intervisibility, visual alignment and the study of non-visible areas.

van Leusen (1998) notes that it is likely that viewshed analysis has received so much attention in recent years because of its potential to escape the environmental determinism trap often levied at GIS practitioners. However there are many other pitfalls for the viewshed practitioner, including the 'tree problem' (Wheatley 1996), the edge effect (Lake *et al.* 1998), curvature of the earth (Ruggles and Medyckyj-Scott 1996; Fisher *et al.* 1997) the significance of distance (Ruggles and Medyckyj-Scott 1996; Wheatley 1996) and one of the topics of this paper, correlation mistaken for causation.

Viewshed analysis is used in this study to address three main questions:

- **Were tombs really located at prominent positions in the landscape?**

- **If so, is there any indication in the nature of the viewshed that the tombs were located to see *from* rather than *to be seen*?**

- **Can the content of the viewshed tell us anything further about the 'unequivocal importance of visibility'?**

In attempting to address these questions specific attention will be drawn to a number of important methodological issues relating to viewshed analysis in archaeology. The intense computational analysis required to generate viewshed data was carried out using the r.cva module, designed for use with the GRASS GIS (see Table 1 for the URLs for these resources). The r.cva module was developed by Dr. M. W. Lake as part of the MAGICAL project directed by Dr. S. J. Mithen (Department of Archaeology, University of Reading, U.K.) and funded by NERC (1995–1998).

3 Prominence of location

'Were tombs really located at prominent positions in the landscape?'

Given the vagaries of many of the statements concerning the prominent location of tombs and their visibility, it is important to investigate whether there is enough evidence to state that Orcadian tombs were preferentially located in prominent positions in the landscape. It may well be true that tombs occupy prominent locations in the landscape, but this may be a mere factor of chance and natural topography, in other words simple correlation, rather than a product of preference or intention. It is also possible that the present day distribution of remains has been significantly biased by later destruction.

Although the *prominence* of any feature of the landscape will inevitably be variable, dependent on both the individual and the location of viewing, it is possible to use viewshed analysis to investigate the relative visibility of particular locations, thereby giving an indication of which locations are likely to be more visible and hence more *prominent* than others. By using 'completeness of viewshed' as an indicator of prominence it is possible to investigate how prominent the tombs are in the landscape. The completeness of viewshed statistic is the size of visible area as a proportion of that which would be visible over a given radius on a completely flat plain, given perfect visibility conditions. Figure 1 shows the cumulative frequency of the completeness of

viewshed values carried out over three distances (2km, 5km and 10km) for a sample of random points and at the location of each of 78 tombs.

There is a clear difference between the results from the chambered cairn viewsheds and from the random sample viewsheds. The results from the chambered cairn viewsheds were compared to those from the random sample viewsheds generated using the same maximum visible distance. In all three cases (viewsheds of 2, 5 and 10km) the difference between the results was statistically significant at a level of 0.01 (significance testing was carried out using the two sample Kolmogorov-Smirnov test). Substantially more tomb viewsheds are more complete than those from the random sample of locations are. There is therefore a pattern, a correlation between the location of chambered cairns and places from which it is possible to see a large proportion of the surrounding landscape. However this does not mean that the tombs were positioned with this in mind. Correlation has been demonstrated but causation or intention is still debatable. It remains to be demonstrated that there is a meaningful relationship between visibility and the intention of the Neolithic tomb builders.

It has already been noted that many other researchers have suggested possible influences on the location of the Orcadian chambered cairns. Examples include overlooking settlement sites, on good agricultural land or on the margin with good and bad land etc. Another pattern in the distribution of chambered cairns in Orkney is their proximity to the coast. Perhaps this is of equal or greater importance than the prominence of their location. Figure 1 shows that there is a higher proportion of more complete viewsheds from cairn locations than from the random locations. One strong reason for this is likely to be that cairns are located on the coast (as is shown in Figure 2) overlooking large areas of flat seascape, while the random points may fall away from the coast with a higher likelihood of undulating terrain blocking or interrupting visibility. This is a very simple demonstration of the risk of attributing importance to visibility simply because it correlates with proximity to the coast. Distance to the sea may be the causal factor while prominence may simply correlate with it.

It is therefore important to test for patterning in visibility while simultaneously taking on board other perhaps more primary and practical influences (elevation, proximity to coast, soil type and quality) which may be correlated. The basic functionality of GIS makes this a relatively pain-

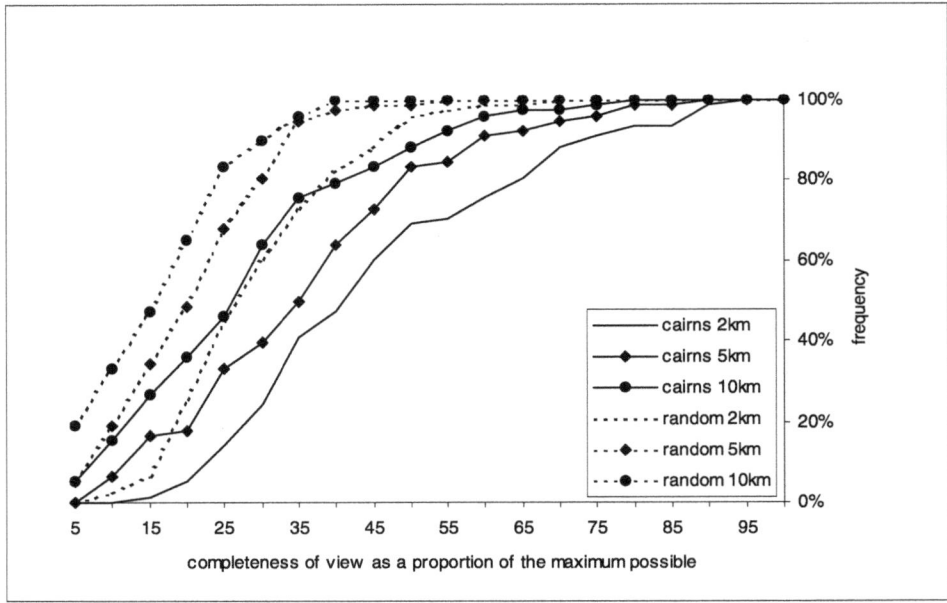

Figure 1: Completeness of view (within 2, 5 and 10km).

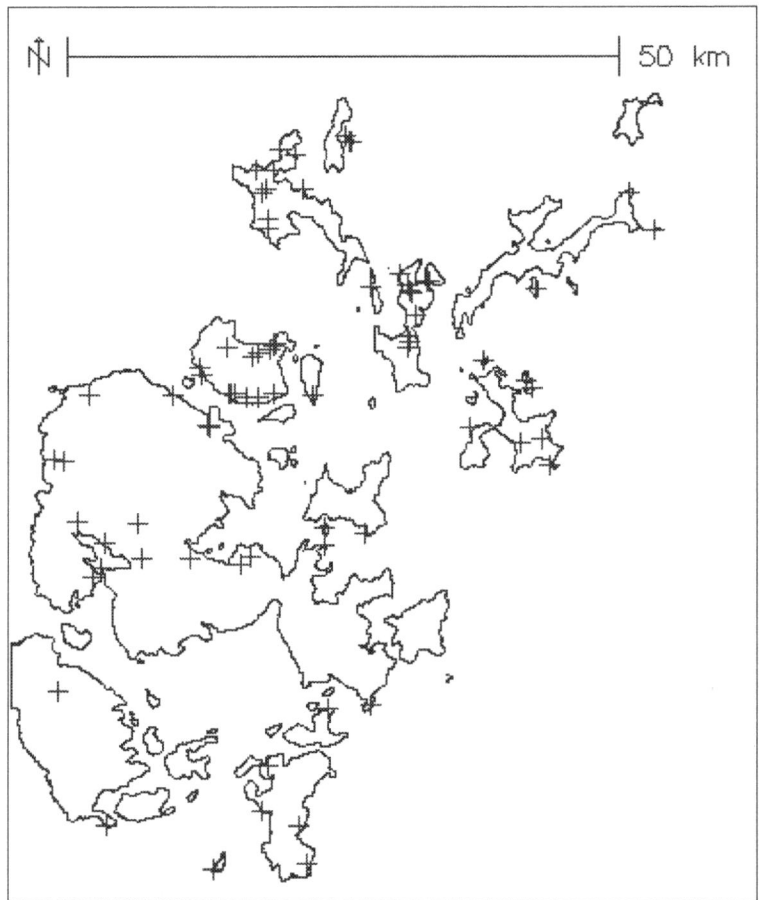

Figure 2: Distribution map of known Neolithic chambered cairns. ©Crown Copyright ED274623

Software	URL	Accessed
GRASS GIS	http://www.baylor.edu/ grass/	15/02/00
GRASS module r.cva	http://www.ucl.ac.uk/archaeology/research/profiles/lake.htm	17/02/00

Table 1: URLs of software resources cited in the text.

less exercise. It is possible to extract the sample of random locations only from areas that have a range of similar attributes to the locations where Neolithic communities built their burial mounds.

In this study a sample of random locations were taken only from areas with the same values as a range of standard environmental/topographical attributes as the tombs (areas under 80m OD. within 500m from the coast and on relatively flat ground). Although only three variables are used they represent many other possible influences such as soil quality (on the low-lying coastal areas), the presence of arable land, proximity to settlements (all of which show a preference for low-lying and coastal areas), differential preservation and destruction. This method accommodates the possibility that the present distribution may have been affected by later destruction. In effect it allows testing for a preference of prominent locations within the patterning already noted. In other words, this method seeks to ascertain whether the known chambered cairns are located in more prominent locations than the random ones, when they too are constrained by other factors (such as those listed above) likely to have played a role in creating the current distribution of tombs. Carrying out this more realistic test does indeed give rather a different result.

Figure 3 shows that in the case of the 2km and 5km maximum visibility there is a significant difference between the archaeological sample and the random sample indicating that even taking other factors into consideration cairns do not seem to be located randomly with regard to visibility. Given that the test has taken other influential factors into consideration this does strongly indicate that visibility was an important influence in locating tombs and is likely to be *more* than a simple correlation phenomenon.

3.1 Why were tombs located in prominent locations?

'Is there any indication in the nature of the viewshed that the tombs were located to see *from* rather than *to be seen*?'

In addressing the first question a rather loose concept of prominence and visibility was used. The logic employed was that points from which one can see a large area are points that can be seen from many other places. By indicating that a larger area is visible from tombs than might be expected by chance (in other words, than is possible from random locations) it has been intimated that the tombs themselves are more visible than might be expected by chance. However as can be seen in Figure 4 these two statements are not necessarily interchangeable. Fraser (1983, 301–2) acknowledges that his work on the location of the chambered cairns assumes a reciprocity of vision that does not necessarily exist. He notes that to distinguish between 'visible from' and 'visibility to' would require "an inordinate amount of work". Fraser continues on to suggest that in his opinion 'visibility to' is the proper avenue of enquiry, although he does not support this further.

Using viewshed analysis it is now possible to distinguish between 'visibility from' and 'visibility to'. It is by exploring the difference between them that I hope to improve our understanding of the location of chambered cairns and help to elucidate the intention behind location selection.

Visiting a number of the Orcadian chambered tombs a number of points are revealed. Firstly it is striking that although they are located in so called prominent places they are not in themselves very visible features in the landscape, while on the other hand the views from the monuments are often spectacular. Secondly it is noteworthy that it is often not possible to see the tombs from very nearby. A non-Orcadian example that demonstrates the same phenomenon is West Kennet Long Barrow. When approaching by the modern access path the mound disappears and only becomes visible a few yards before reaching it. Finally standing at the Orcadian tombs the predominant orientation of view is almost always offshore.

By examining these observations in a quantitative manner it is possible to begin to explore the intentionality behind the choice of a prominent location. It has already been noted that it is not strictly accurate to equate the viewshed area with the area from which the location is visible. However, by reducing the elevation of the viewer to 0m (and raising the surrounding land by the av-

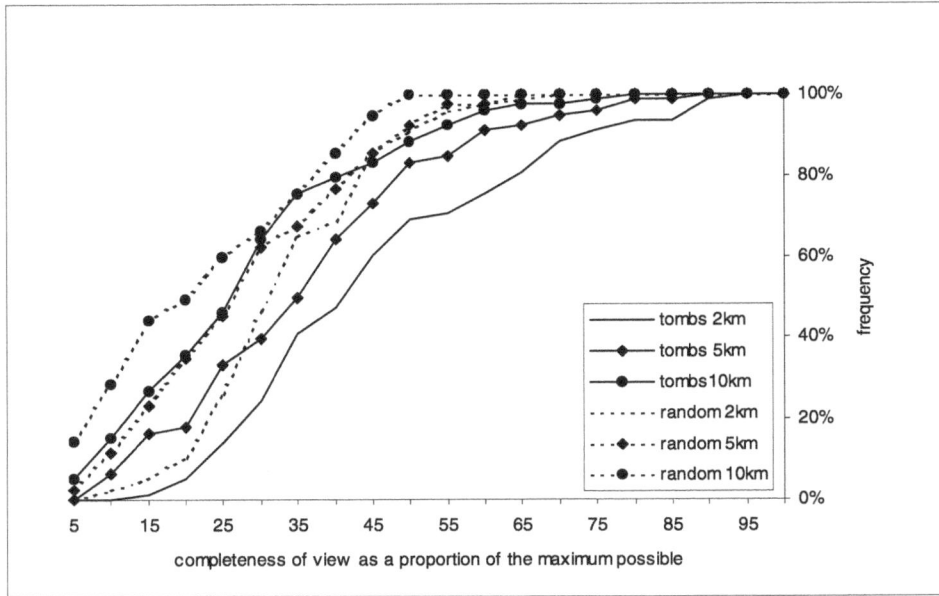

Figure 3: Completeness of view from the sample of tombs and from a constrained random sample of points.

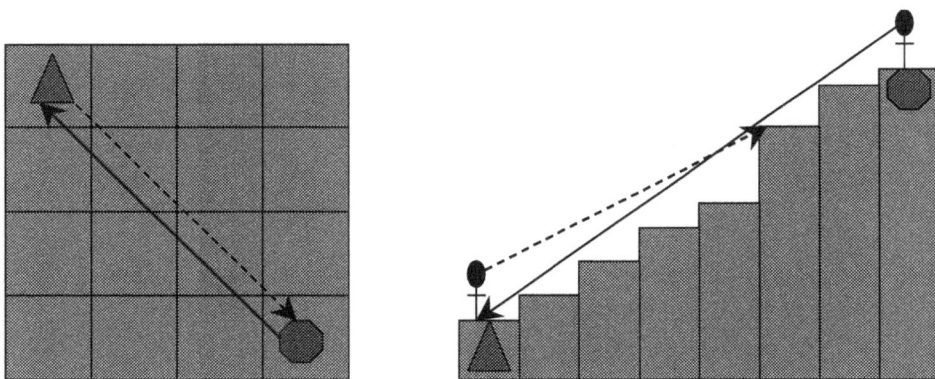

Figure 4: Areas visible from a particular location are not interchangeable with areas from which that location is itself visible.

erage height of a person, 1.75m) and only taking the visible land area into account it is possible to simulate locations from which any one point (cairn location or random point) is visible. By comparing the nature of the viewsheds *from* the sites and those that simulated visibility *to* the site it is possible to start to address the question of intentionality.

In Figure 5 it is firstly evident that the areas from which the tombs are actually visible is vastly reduced from that which can be seen from the tomb. In fact using 5km as an optimistic estimate of the maximum distance over which a tomb is visible, from 66% of the present day Orkney land area it would not be possible to see a surviving chambered cairn (Figure 6).

Secondly, within a given radius there is a tendency for a large proportion of the visible area to fall within the sea (Figure 7). Due to the fundamental nature of operating in an island environment, the proportion of sea visible increases as does the maximum distance of visibility (as the graph shows). However, even using a 2km radius, over 65% of the visible area is seascape from 50% of the tomb locations, while only 33% of the background sample has such extensive seascapes (Figure 8). It therefore seems that it was of *more* importance to locate burial places with extensive views over water than over land, from this it can be inferred that it is visibility *from* the burial mound that was more important than many people being able to see it from many places.

Visiting a number of the Orcadian tombs the manipulation of visibility close to the burial mound is evident. In many cases the tombs are if anything not visible from the immediately surrounding land. For example many of the tombs on the south coast of Rousay (much studied by Childe and Renfrew amongst others) are generally not visible from the low-lying coastal lands until within a couple of hundred metres of them.

When the observations based on quantitative tests are added to those made on the ground it seems that it was not overly important for the living communities to be able to see to the burial mounds while going about their daily activities on the islands. Rather it seems that it was visibility from the chambered cairn that influenced their location. If anything it is perhaps possible that tombs could have been located to be invisible at closer proximity (Woodman forthcoming a).

3.2 The nature of visibility from tombs

'Can the content of the viewshed tell us anything further about the "unequivocal importance of visibility"?'

Intervisibility between Neolithic burial mounds has been the subject of a number of studies in recent years. It is suggested that intervisibility was particularly sought in certain areas, for example the Salisbury Plain area (Wheatley 1995), while in other areas this is not a concern, for example the Avebury (Wheatley 1996) and Danebury areas (Lock and Harris 1996). The Orcadian tombs do seem to have a higher frequency of intervisibility than would be expected by chance alone. Figure 9 shows that there are fewer tombs from which no other tomb can be seen than is the case for the (constrained) random sample. Also there are more tombs from which 2 and 3 other tombs are visible than is the case for random sample. But again we must ask is this causal, or is intervisibility merely correlated with larger viewsheds? Interestingly this does not seem to be the case. Tombs from which two and three other tombs can be seen tend to have smaller viewsheds than those from which only one or no other tomb can be seen (Figure 10). It could therefore be said that tombs were located with some regard to lines of sight to other tombs illustrating some degree of connection across the landscape.

It has already been demonstrated above that there is a clear pattern for tombs to be located within sight of water. This is even the case for seemingly inland cairns such Maes Howe itself (with a view over the inland Loch of Harray and the sea Loch of Stenness). The Dwarfie Stane (an unusual rock cut tomb) located almost in the middle of the island of Hoy, is another dramatic example of this. The tomb lies at the side of a deep U-shaped valley cutting across the island yet there is a clear view north towards the Orkney mainland, over the Hoy Sound (Figure 11). It is of note that if the tomb were any further along the valley (to the south or west) this view would no longer be possible. Interestingly a similar pattern has been noted by Fisher *et al.* (1997) concerning Bronze Age cairns on Mull. Perhaps this tells us something of the beliefs of later prehistoric peoples. Indeed Richard Bradley's (1997) study of the location of Swedish Bronze Age rock art located between the sea and burial mounds may be of relevance here. The artwork depicts boats and footprints and Bradley suggests that it acts as a passage from one to the other. So perhaps water formed an important part of the passage to the next life. The spirit passing from

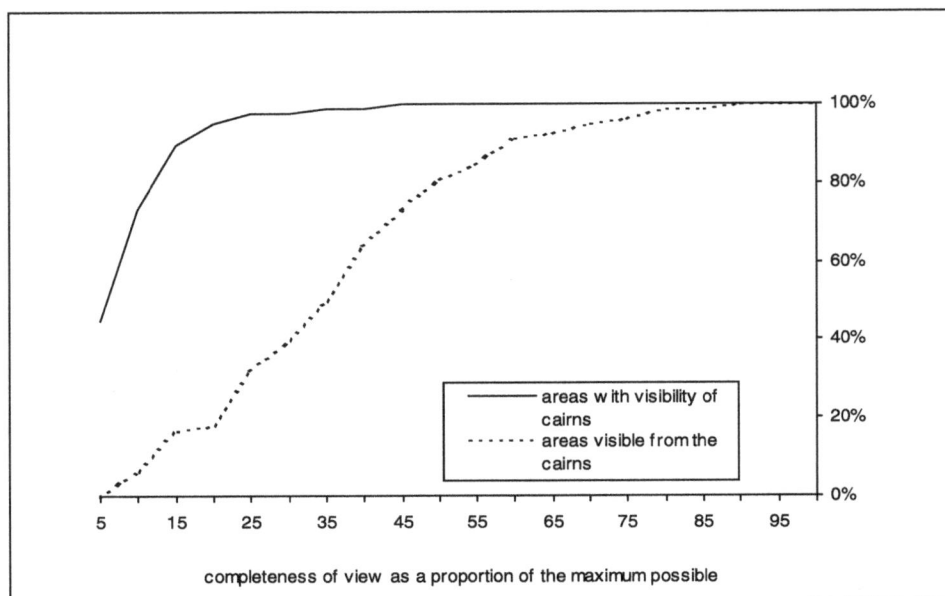

Figure 5: Areas 'visible from' and areas with 'visibility to' cairns.

the tomb (in the case of the Swedish Bronze Age examples over the artwork) into the water. In the case of the Orcadian farmers it could be that it was important for the spirit to see the route to the next life from the resting place of the tomb.

Finally, do different sorts of tombs have different sorts of visibility? For statistical purposes all the Orcadian chambered tombs were lumped together as one group in this study, however they do actually take a number of different forms and cover an extensive time span. Two main categories are distinguished: the Orkney-Cromarty type (including those with tripartite, stalled and Bookan type chambers) and the later Maes Howe type. It is unfortunate from a statistical point of view that the sample of Maes Howe tombs is so small (numbering only 12 in comparison to 49 Orkney-Cromarty types). Nevertheless we can note a slight indication that the Maes Howe tombs do not have the same preference for large views over water (Figure 12).

4 Conclusion

Viewshed analysis is seen by some as a means of moving away from analysis within an 'objective' geographical space where our viewpoint is external to the phenomenon, towards a more subjective space, allowing us to model perception and cognition and move closer to participating from within the experience of past peoples (Gaffney et al. 1996; van Leusen 1998). This is an admi-

ral goal, but at a more mundane level there are a number of methodological issues that must be dealt with before it is wise to travel too far down this path.

This research has highlighted a number of points both about the use of GIS (viewshed analysis in particular) in archaeology and about the distribution of Orcadian Neolithic chambered cairns.

Two important methodological points are made in relation to the application of viewshed analysis to the archaeological record. Firstly, that GIS practitioners in archaeology need to move beyond pattern recognition (identification of correlations) towards elucidating the causal factors involved. In this study the aim was to try to gain an insight into the intention behind the location of the cairns. Given that there are many other likely influences on location the significance of visibility was tested within the bounds of other likely influences. Although there does seem to be a clear pattern of locations close to the coast being favoured for cairn building, visibility does nevertheless seem to have been part of the location selection criteria.

The second methodological point made here is that areas visible from a specified location and areas from which that same location is visible are not one and the same thing. In other words the viewshed is not reversible. One of the starting points for this study was recognition of the variety of statements about prominence and visibility in relation to the Orcadian (and other)

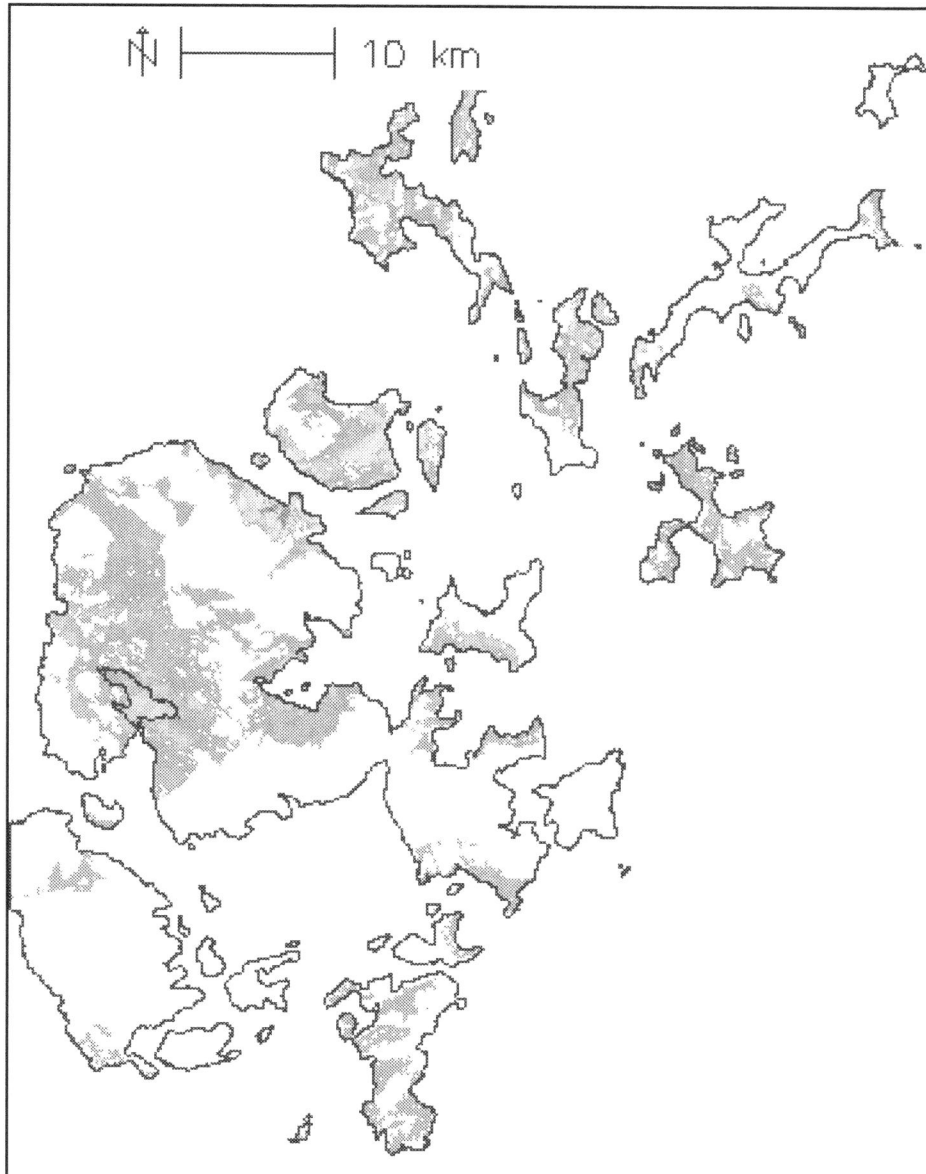

Figure 6: Locations from which it is possible to see one or more cairns. ©Crown Copyright ED274623

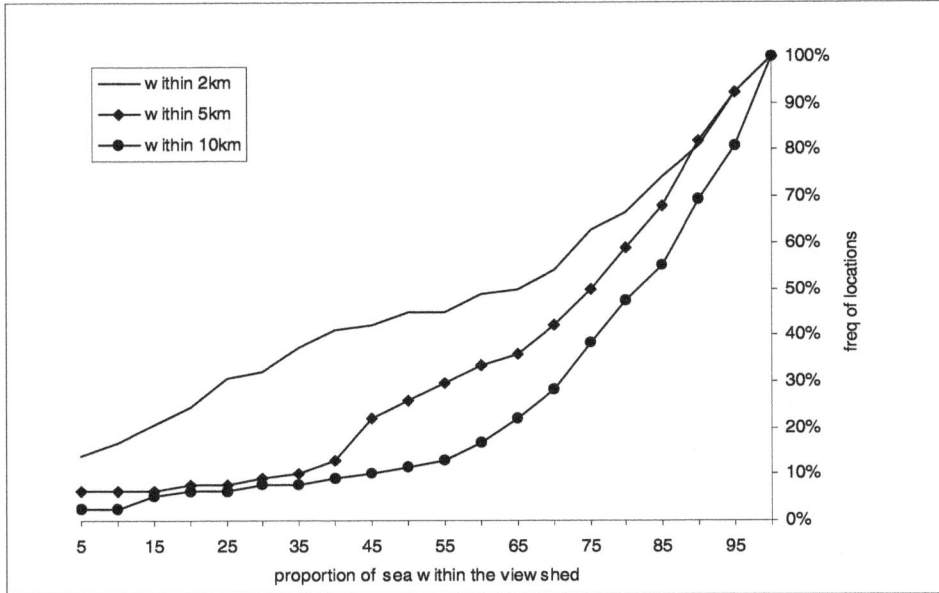

Figure 7: Proportion of viewshed containing sea.

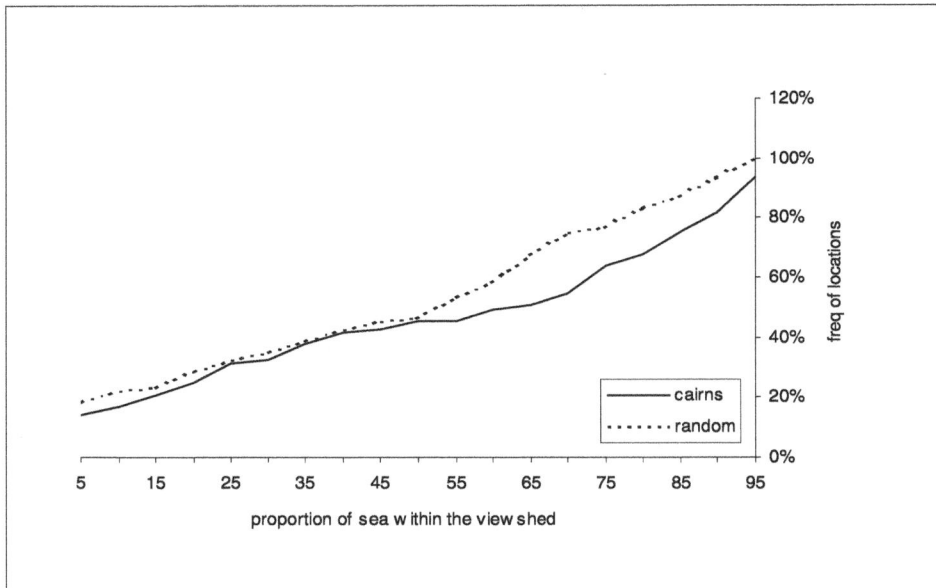

Figure 8: Proportion of viewshed containing sea within a maximum distance of 2km.

100

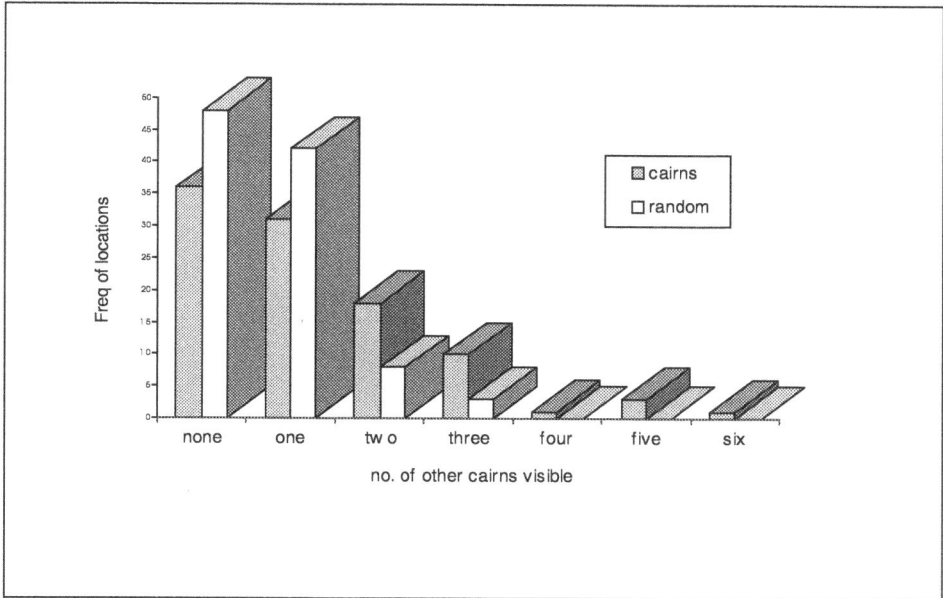

Figure 9: Intervisibility between cairns.

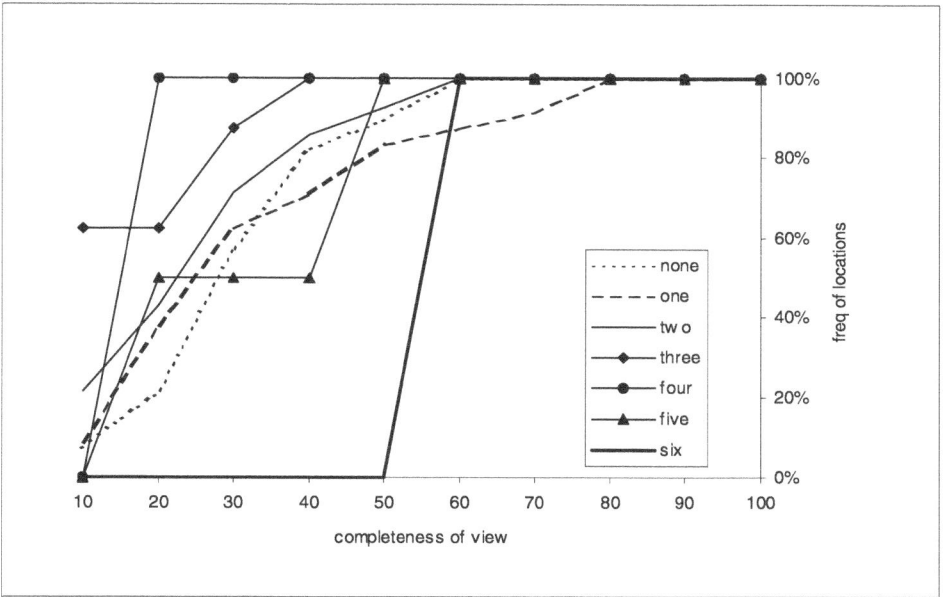

Figure 10: Intervisibility compared to viewshed size.

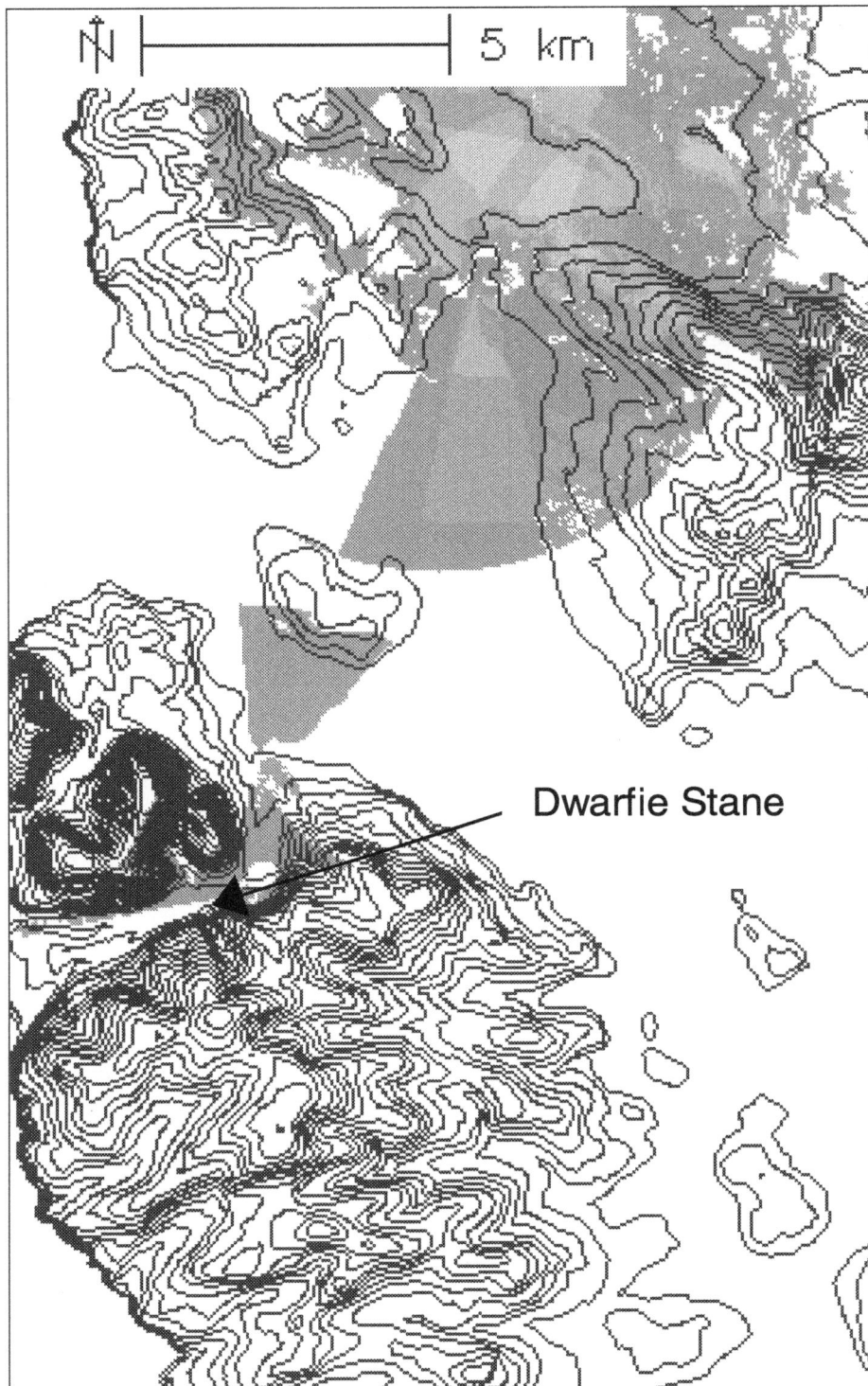

Figure 11: Viewshed from the Dwarfie Stane. ©Crown Copyright ED274623

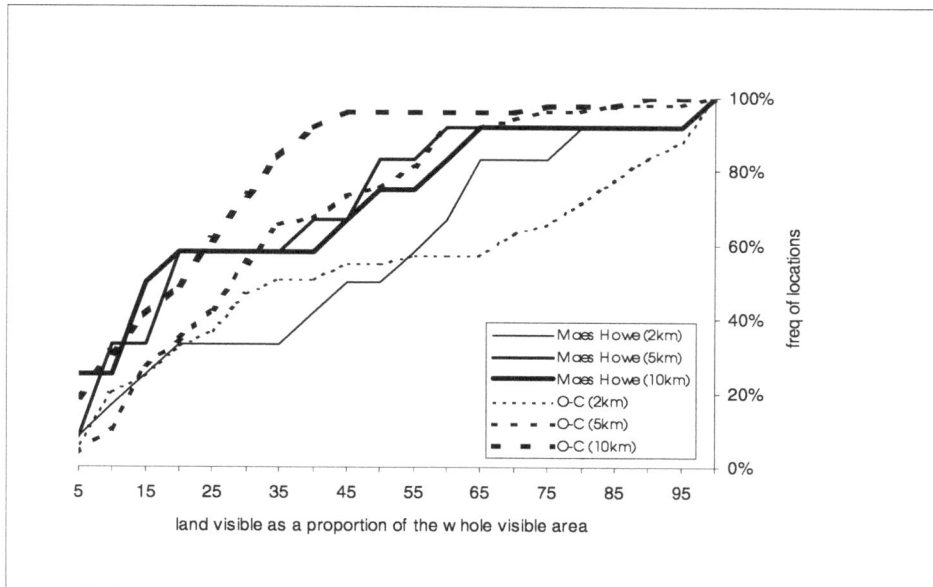

Figure 12: Proportion of land visible with viewsheds from Orkney-Cromarty and Maes Howe tombs.

chambered tombs. Although there is apparently widespread agreement that there is some relationship, there has been less agreement about its exact nature and significance. The aim of this work was to look more closely at the prominence of (visibility to) and visibility (view) from the chambered cairns in order to gain an insight into the possible intentions that lie behind the positioning of the burial mounds.

The application of viewshed analysis to the existing record of Orcadian chambered cairns has indeed made it possible to add a further facet to our understanding of the tombs and the people who built them. The results of this study indicate that the chambered tombs of Orkney are located with regard to visibility, and it is visibility from the tomb that appears to be of overriding concern. Proximity to and visibility over areas of water seems to have an importance. It is possible that this is a concern that is also important in relation to Bronze Age cairns in Sweden (Bradley 1997) and on the Isle of Mull (Fisher *et al.* 1997). Preliminary work on other Neolithic burial mounds elsewhere in Scotland show a similar pattern (Woodman forthcoming b).

It can also be noted that a certain level of intervisibility exists between the Orcadian tombs, possibly indicating a degree of connection across the landscape between the places of the dead. The differences between the nature of the view from the Orkney-Cromarty cairns and the later Maes Howe type burials could indicate that the meaning associated with the visibility of tombs

changed through time in this area.

5 Postscript

Since this research was carried out r.cva has been further developed and is now a comprehensive module for viewshed analysis. It now offers the facility to carry out analysis from a site_list file, a random sample of points, or from a systematic sample over a specified proportion of the landscape. It also allows visibility of locations as well as the view from a point to be analysed. The code for this software is available from its developer (Dr. M. W. Lake at his World-Wide-Web site, see Table 1 for the URL).

6 Acknowledgements

This research would not have been possible without the development of the viewshed module r.cva. Initial work on which was carried out by Dr. M. W. Lake under the auspices of the MAGICAL project. I am also grateful to him for the many discussions of the results from the analysis and his encouragement in writing this paper.

References

[1] Allen, K. M. S. 1990. Modelling early historic trade in the eastern Great Lakes using geographical information systems. In

K. M. S. Allen, S. W. Green and E. B. W. Zubrow, (eds.), *Interpreting Space: GIS and Archaeology*, pp. 319–29. London, Taylor & Francis.

[2] Allen, K. M. S., Green, S. W. and Zubrow, E. B. W., (eds.) 1990. *Interpreting Space: GIS and Archaeology*. London, Taylor & Francis.

[3] Bradley, R. 1997. Death by water: boats and footprints in the rock art of western Sweden. *Oxford Journal of Archaeology*, 16(3):315–24.

[4] Childe, V. G. 1942. The chambered cairns of Rousay. *Antiquaries Journal*, 22:139–42.

[5] Childe, V. G. 1952. Re-excavation of the chambered cairn of Quoyness, Sanday, on behalf of the Ministry of Works in 1961–52. *Proceedings of the Society of Antiquaries of Scotland*, 86:121–39.

[6] Childe, V. G. 1956. Maes Howe. *Proceedings of the Society of Antiquaries of Scotland*, 88:155–66.

[7] Crumley, C. L. and Marquardt, W. H. 1990. Landscape: a unifying concept in regional analysis. In K. M. S. Allen, S. W. Green and E. B. W. Zubrow, (eds.), *Interpreting Space: GIS and Archaeology*, pp. 73–79. London, Taylor & Francis.

[8] Davidson, D. 1979. The Orcadian environment and cairn location. In C. Renfrew, (ed.), *Investigations in Orkney*, pp. 9–20. London, Society of Antiquaries of London Research Report 38.

[9] Davidson, J. L. and Henshall, A. S. 1989. *The Chambered cairns of Orkney*. Edinburgh, Edinburgh University Press.

[10] Fisher, P., Farrelly, C., Maddocks, A. and Ruggles, C. 1997. Spatial analysis of visible areas from the Bronze Age cairns of Mull. *Journal of Archaeological Science*, 24:581–92.

[11] Fraser, D. 1983. *Land and Society in Neolithic Orkney*. Oxford, British Archaeological Reports Series 117.

[12] Fraser, D. 1988. The orientation of visibility from the chambered cairns of Eday, Orkney. In C. Ruggles, (ed.), *Records in Stone*. Cambridge, Cambridge University Press.

[13] Gaffney, V., Stancic, Z. and Watson, H. 1995. The impact of GIS on archaeology: a personal perspective. In G. Lock and Z. Stancic, (eds.), *Archaeology and Geographic Information Systems*, pp. 211–30. London, Taylor & Francis.

[14] Gaffney, V. and van Leusen, P. M. 1995. GIS, environmental determinism and archaeology. In G. Lock and Z. Stancic, (eds.), *Archaeology and Geographic Information Systems*, pp. 367–82. London, Taylor & Francis.

[15] Gaffney, V. L., Stancic, Z. and Watson, H. 1996. Moving from Catchments to Cognition: Tentative Steps Toward a Larger Archaeological Context for GIS. In M. Aldenderfer and H. Maschner, (eds.), *Anthropology, Space, and Geographic Information Systems*, pp. 132–54. Oxford, Oxford University Press.

[16] Green, S. W. 1990. Sorting out settlement in southeastern Ireland: landscape archaeology and Geographic Information Systems. In K. M. S. Allen, S. W. Green and E. B. W. Zubrow, (eds.), *Interpreting Space: GIS and Archaeology*, pp. 356–63. London, Taylor & Francis.

[17] Harris, T. M. and Lock, G. R. 1995. Towards an evaluation of GIS in European archaeology: the past, present and future of theory and explanation. In G. Lock and Z. Stancic, (eds.), *Archaeology and Geographic Information Systems*, pp. 349–66. London, Taylor & Francis.

[18] Hasenstab, R. J. and Resnick, B. 1990. GIS in historical predictive modelling: the Fort Drum Project. In K. M. S. Allen, S. W. Green and E. B. W. Zubrow, (eds.), *Interpreting Space: GIS and Archaeology*, pp. 284–306. London, Taylor & Francis.

[19] Hedges, J. W. 1983. *Isbister; a chambered tomb in Orkney*. 115. Oxford, British Archaeological Reports.

[20] Hodder, I. 1982. *Symbols in Action*. Cambridge, Cambridge University Press.

[21] Lake, M. W., Woodman, P. E. and Mithen, S. J. 1998. Tailoring GIS software for archaeological applications: an example concerning viewshed analysis. *Journal of Archaeological Science*, 25:27–38.

[22] Llobera, M. 1996. Exploring the topography of mind: GIS, social space and archaeology. *Antiquity*, 70:612–22.

[23] Lock, G. R. and Harris, T. M. 1996. Danebury revisited: an English Iron Age hillfort in a digital landscape. In M. S. Aldenderfer and H. D. G. Maschner, (eds.), *Anthropology, Space, and Geographic Information Systems*, pp. 214–40. Oxford, Oxford University Press.

[24] Maschner, H. D. G. 1996. Geographic Information systems in Archaeology. In M. Aldenderfer and H. D. G. Maschner, (eds.), *Anthropology, Space, and Geographic Information Systems*, pp. 1–21. Oxford, Oxford University Press.

[25] Petrie, G. 1863. The Picts' Houses in the Orkneys. *Archaeological Journal*, 20:32–37.

[26] Renfrew, A. C. 1973. *Before Civilization: the radiocarbon revolution and Prehistoric Europe*. London, Cape.

[27] Renfrew, A. C. 1979. *Investigations in Orkney*. London, Society of Antiquaries of London Research Report 38.

[28] Ritchie, P. R. 1959. A chambered cairn at Isbister, South Ronaldsay. *Proceedings of the Society of Antiquaries of Scotland*, 92:25–32.

[29] Ruggles, C. L. N. and Medyckyj-Scott, D. J. 1996. Site location, landscape visibility, and symbolic astronomy: a Scottish case study. In M. Aldenderfer and H. Maschner, (eds.), *Anthropology, Space, and Geographic Information Systems*, pp. 127–146. Oxford, Oxford University Press.

[30] Savage, S. H. 1990. Modeling the Late Archaic Social Landscape. In K. M. S. Allen, S. W. Green and E. B. W. Zubrow, (eds.), *Interpreting Space: GIS and Archaeology*, pp. 330–55. London, Taylor & Francis.

[31] van Leusen, M. 1999. Viewshed and cost surface analysis using GIS: cartographic modelling in cell-based GIS II. In J. A. Barcelo, I. Briz and A. Vila, (eds.), *New Techniques for Old Times. CAA98: Computer Applications and Quantitative Methods in Archaeology. Proceedings of the 26th Conference, Barcelona 1998*, pp. 215–223. BAR International Series 757.

[32] Warren, R. E. 1990. Predictive modelling of archaeological site location: a case study in the Midwest. In K. M. S. Allen, S. W. Green and E. B. W. Zubrow, (eds.), *Interpreting Space: GIS and Archaeology*, pp. 201–15. London, Taylor & Francis.

[33] Wheatley, D. 1995. Cumulative viewshed analysis: a GIS-based method for investigating intervisibility, and its archaeological application. In G. Lock and Z. Stancic, (eds.), *Archaeology and Geographic Information Systems*, pp. 171–86. London, Taylor & Francis.

[34] Wheatley, D. 1996. The Use of GIS to Understand Regional Variation in earlier Neolithic Wessex. In M. Aldenderfer and H. Maschner, (eds.), *Anthropology, Space, and Geographic Information Systems*, pp. 75–103. Oxford, Oxford University Press.

[35] Woodman, P. E. forthcoming a. Neolithic death views or life views: an investigation of the nature of visual communication with Orcadian Neolithic chambered tombs.

[36] Woodman, P. E. forthcoming b. Water and death: a view on Neolithic death belief.

[37] Zubrow, E. B. W. 1990. Modelling and prediction with Geographic Information Systems: a demographic example from prehistoric and historic New York. In K. M. S. Allen, S. W. Green and E. B. W. Zubrow, (eds.), *Interpreting Space: GIS and Archaeology*, pp. 307–18. London, Taylor & Francis.

www.ingramcontent.com/pod-product-compliance
Lightning Source LLC
Chambersburg PA
CBHW051303270326
41926CB00030B/4705